THE BRIDE PRICE

There's an old saying that 'Love will always find a way'. But is that true? What happens if love is forbidden by customs and tradition, and so gets caught in a battle between the old world and the new? How can love find a way then? Tradition is not an easy enemy to fight.

Aku-nna is a young girl, and has much to learn about the ways of the world. After her father's death, she goes to live in a small town where the old traditions are strong. Aku-nna has no sisters to advise her; her brother, Nna-nndo, is too young; her mother, Ma Blackie, is too busy with her new life. Only Chike, the schoolteacher, is kind and gentle towards the shy, lonely girl.

But Aku-nna comes from a proud, free-born family, and Chike is from a family who were once slaves . . .

NIGERIA

The main characters in this story are Ibos (also spelt Igbos), most of whom live to the east of the great Niger River (see the map on the next page). Lagos, the capital city of Nigeria since colonial times, is in the west, where the Yoruba people live. Aku-nna and her family lived first in Lagos, and then in their 'hometown', Ibuza, a small Ibo town near the Niger.

At the time of this story, in the late 1950s, Nigeria had been under British rule for about fifty years. Nigeria became independent in 1960.

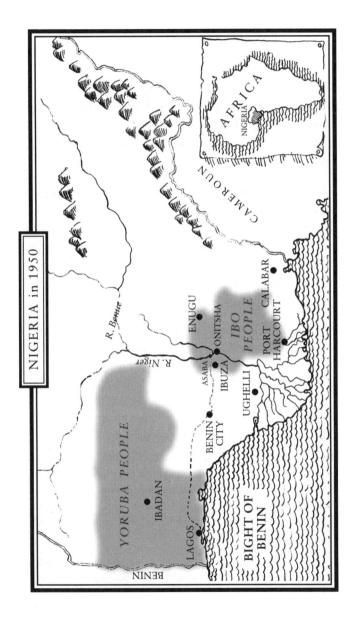

NIGERIA in 1950

AFRICA

NIGERIA

CAMEROUN

R. Benue

R. Niger

ENUGU

ONITSHA

IBO PEOPLE

PORT CALABAR

ASABA

IBUZA

HARCOURT

UGHELLI

BENIN CITY

YORUBA PEOPLE

IBADAN

LAGOS

BIGHT OF BENIN

BENIN

OXFORD BOOKWORMS LIBRARY

Human Interest

The Bride Price

Stage 5 (1800 headwords)

Series Editor: Jennifer Bassett
Founder Editor: Tricia Hedge
Activities Editors: Jennifer Bassett and Christine Lindop

BUCHI EMECHETA

The Bride Price

Retold by
Rosemary Border

OXFORD UNIVERSITY PRESS

OXFORD
UNIVERSITY PRESS

Great Clarendon Street, Oxford OX2 6DP

Oxford University Press is a department of the University of Oxford.
It furthers the University's objective of excellence in research, scholarship,
and education by publishing worldwide in

Oxford New York

Auckland Cape Town Dar es Salaam Hong Kong Karachi
Kuala Lumpur Madrid Melbourne Mexico City Nairobi
New Delhi Shanghai Taipei Toronto

With offices in

Argentina Austria Brazil Chile Czech Republic France Greece
Guatemala Hungary Italy Japan Poland Portugal Singapore
South Korea Switzerland Thailand Turkey Ukraine Vietnam

OXFORD and OXFORD ENGLISH are registered trade marks of
Oxford University Press in the UK and in certain other countries

ISBN 978 0 19 479218 9

Printed in China

ACKNOWLEDGEMENTS
Illustrated by: Deborah Loftus
Map by: Martin Ursell

Word count (main text): 22,620 words

I

Distributed By:
Grass Roots Press
Toll Free: 1-888-303-3213
Fax: (780) 413-6582
Web Site: www.grassrootsbooks.net

CONTENTS

PEOPLE IN THIS STORY

Ezekiel Odia

Ma Blackie, *his wife*

Aku-nna, *their daughter (her name means 'Father's Wealth')*

Nna-nndo, *their son (his name means 'Father is the Shelter')*

Uncle Uche
Uncle Joseph } *the children's uncles*

Aunt Uzo
Aunt Mary } *the children's aunts*

Dick, *a houseboy in the apartment house in Lagos*

Okonkwo Odia, *elder brother of Ezekiel, uncle of Aku-nna and Nna-nndo, and second husband of Ma Blackie*

Ngbeke, *Okonkwo's Number One wife*

Ogugua, *their daughter, and cousin of Aku-nna and Nna-nndo*

Iloba
Osenekwu } *their sons, and cousins of Aku-nna and Nna-nndo*

Chike Ofulue, *the schoolteacher*
Ofulue, *Chike's father* } *the 'slave' family*

Ben Adegor, *Chike's friend*

Rose, *Ben's wife*

The Obidi family

Okoboshi, *the Obidis' son*

Father Osborne, *in charge of the church school*

Zik, *the dancing teacher*

1

Father Goes Away

Aku-nna turned the key in the lock and pushed open the door of her family's one-room apartment in Lagos, Nigeria. To her surprise her father was standing there in his work clothes, with his hat in his hand. He looked like a criminal who had been caught stealing.

Aku-nna and her brother Nna-nndo stared at him. 'You ought to be at work,' their silent looks said. 'You ought to be at the factory.' But their father did not offer any explanation.

Nna-nndo was eleven. He was a tall boy for his age. At school he was just starting to write with ink, and he was proud of this. However, although he was very clever in other ways, Nna-nndo was very slow at book work. There was always ink on his fingers and on his school uniform. Sometimes he rubbed ink on his woolly hair. When people asked him why, he always replied, 'Ink makes my hair blacker!' He loved a joke, just like their mother, Ma Blackie.

Ma Blackie was a huge woman, as tall and straight as a tree, with extremely black, shiny skin. She was always smiling. But behind her smile Ma Blackie had a problem. She seemed unable to have another baby.

In 1945, the local men came back from the war in Burma. All their wives had babies soon afterwards – all except Ma Blackie. Now, five years later, there was still no sign of another child. Her husband, Ezekiel Odia, had sent her to all the native doctors that he could afford, but without success. At last she decided to make the two-hundred-mile journey to her home town of Ibuza. There she asked the river goddess to send her a baby.

While their mother was away, Aku-nna and Nna-nndo had to take care of themselves and their father. He worked hard at the factory, building railway engines, and his job was important to him.

He was a small man with a small voice. People often wondered why he had married such a big woman. The answer was simple. Like most men of his age, Ezekiel had married his bride when she was still a young girl. But Ezekiel's bride did not stop growing! They were a happy couple and the difference in their height did not seem to matter, except that when Ezekiel wanted to say something serious to his wife, he had a habit of standing on his toes.

Today the children were surprised to see their father at home. There he stood, anxiously turning his old hat over and over in his hands. Aku-nna came nearer to him. She was only thirteen, but she knew that all was not well in her family. She often heard the other women talking about Ma Blackie's childlessness. She often heard her parents arguing too. Her father went on and on in his small sad voice, reminding his wife how much she had cost him.

'I paid double the normal bride price for you,' he told her. 'And we were married in church. But what have you given me – just one son!'

He did not speak of Aku-nna. She was only a girl. Also,

2

she was too thin. Her parents were ashamed of their bony, unhealthy-looking daughter. And that was not all. Aku-nna was often ill. If there was any sickness or fever in their street, Aku-nna always caught it at once. Often her mother begged her to decide once and for all whether she was going to live or die.

'If there's anything I hate,' she said again and again, 'it's an *ogbanje* – a "living dead"!'

Ezekiel Odia often felt sorry for his daughter. She looked like him, and she was like him in other ways too. She was small, and not at all dark. Her skin was a light milk-chocolate colour. Her eyes were large and shining. When she was happy and excited, they shone like stars. When she was sad, their light disappeared.

At her birth, her father named her Aku-nna, which means 'Father's wealth', because he was thinking of the bride price that she would fetch. To him that was something to look forward to, and Aku-nna was determined not to disappoint her father. She planned to marry a wealthy man who could afford an expensive bride price.

'I will not leave my father's house without all the proper ceremonies,' she thought, 'One for the beautiful goddess of Ibuza, and one for the white man's god in church. Then my father will call up the spirits of his great-great-grandparents and ask them to guide us.'

But on this burning-hot day Aku-nna forgot all about her bride price and felt a new sympathy towards her father. She moved nearer to him, sharing his anxiety.

Then he spoke. 'They want me to go to the hospital for a check-up. I shall be home for the evening meal.'

3

The children looked down at their father's painful foot. 'That stupid foot,' Aku-nna said to herself. 'It always gives poor Father a lot of trouble.'

It was the effect of the war. Her uncles had told her that. 'The white men could not fight in Burma,' they told her. 'It was too hot and wet for them. So they sent West African soldiers instead. Your father was lucky to come home alive. Many African soldiers died – but not from the bombs. They died of disease and fever and poisonous insects.'

Her father never talked about it, but his wounded foot often swelled up, particularly during the rainy season. The factory doctor did his best, and the native doctors asked the spirits to make the foot well again, but still it sometimes swelled up. Now it had begun to trouble Ezekiel again, and the other foot was starting to swell too. But today he was wearing his work shoes, and his feet did not look too bad.

'So why,' wondered Aku-nna, 'does Father seem so unhappy? He says he's only going to the hospital for a check-up. He'll be back for his evening meal. So why is he looking so anxious, so disturbed?'

Aku-nna did not ask her father this aloud. That is not the way well-brought-up Nigerian children behave. Nigerian children respect their parents and do not question them. But the anxiety was still there. Something was very wrong, and she knew it.

She laid her small hand on his and said, 'I'm going to make you hot soup and yams, just the way you like them. So, Father, please hurry home and enjoy your evening meal while it's hot!'

Ezekiel smiled lovingly at his daughter. For a moment the sad look on his face disappeared.

'Thank you, little daughter, but don't tire yourself out.' He put his hat on his shaved head. 'The key to the big cupboard is in my grey trousers. If you want any money, take it from the big cupboard. But spend it very carefully.'

The children did not understand why their father was so worried, and they were afraid to ask. Clearly he did not wish to discuss the matter further. He became businesslike, like someone preparing for a final departure. His work-blackened hands touched this and that, picking things up and putting them down again. He told them to be good children, and to respect all adults. He told them to make him proud of them, because he cared for them, because they were his life. At last he went to the door.

'I have to go now,' he said, and added, 'Always remember that you are mine.' His small lips were trembling and it seemed to the children that he was trying desperately not to cry. Helplessly they watched him. He touched each child softly on the head, and went out of the door.

The children followed him. They wanted to beg him to wait. But Ezekiel did not wait. He hurried like a man who is called by the gods . . . He must obey, or be lost for ever.

The children watched him go. Ezekiel crossed the dirt road in front of the house in which they had their small apartment. A lorry loaded with wood came slowly past him. It blew up a cloud of dust that covered Ezekiel. He did not turn to see if the children were watching him. He just walked on. The dust from the lorry hid him from sight,

5

and when the dust blew away, Ezekiel had disappeared.

The children watched the empty road for a while. Then they began to feel hungry, and decided to go in and eat.

They remembered their father's words: 'Always remember that you are mine.'

2

A Death in the Family

The evening meal was ready, but Ezekiel did not come home. 'Soon it will be dark,' thought Aku-nna. 'If Father doesn't come home soon, I'll tell the neighbours. Then they will take care of us.'

She sat on the veranda outside the house, watching and waiting for her father. Then she saw Uncle Uche and Uncle Joseph coming towards her. She knew that her father did not like them. Uncle Uche was the laziest man in town, and Uncle Joseph never stopped talking about other people's business. But she was so glad to see two adults that she jumped up and ran to greet them.

'How are you?' she said. 'My brother is still out playing. Father will punish him when he comes back.'

She smiled, but the uncles did not smile back. They looked rather serious. But that was their business, and Aku-nna did not ask questions. She showed them the good, hot soup and the yams that she had cooked for her father.

Uncle Uche sat down tiredly. 'You've done very well,' he said.

Aku-nna sat on the veranda, watching and waiting for her father.

Uncle Joseph looked at her a little anxiously. 'I'm thirsty,' he said.

Aku-nna hurried to the shelf behind the curtain and fetched her mother's best glass. She poured some water from the big water cooler and gave Uncle Joseph the glass. He drank quickly and asked for more. 'I hope Uncle Uche won't want any,' she thought. 'If he does, there'll be no cool water for Father when he comes home.'

But when Uncle Uche spoke, he did not ask for water.

'Your father isn't coming home tonight. He's going to stay in hospital for a while. They want to find out why his feet are swelling like that. I'll look after you and your brother while he's away.'

Aku-nna opened her mouth and closed it again. 'Father didn't tell me the truth,' she said to herself. 'He said he'd be back for the evening meal. Why did he lie to me, and tell Uncle Uche the truth?'

She looked up at Uncle Uche, and she saw for the first time that his eyes looked red and sore. He spoke gently to her, telling her that the hospital was nothing to be afraid of. But he and Uncle Joseph both seemed near to tears.

Three weeks went by, and still Ezekiel had not come home from hospital. Ma Blackie heard that her husband was ill, and sent a message from Ibuza asking what was happening. But her family in Lagos decided not to tell her the whole truth. They sent a message back telling her not to worry. 'Your children are being well looked after,' they said. 'Ezekiel will be in hospital for a day or two, but he will be home very soon. Your business is with the river goddess.

Don't worry about your children – they are in safe hands.'
So Ma Blackie stayed in Ibuza and concentrated on asking
for another child.

'Father has been away exactly three weeks,' thought Aku-
nna as she sat on the veranda. She wondered when she
would see her parents again. She missed them both very
much. For a short time she had enjoyed 'playing house', but
she soon became tired of it. 'Why can't things be the way
they used to be?' she thought. 'Everything has changed so
much.'

The sun was hanging like a huge red ball in the sky.
Whistles blew at the nearby factory. It was four o'clock and
the workers were on their way home. The wives and
daughters of other families in the house picked up their pots
and their yams and hurried towards the kitchen that
everyone shared.

This kitchen was a large room with sixteen small wood-
burning stoves. There was a stove for each family. Each
cook lit the stove, then cooked the food in a pot on the
burning wood. Aku-nna had no father or husband to cook
for, so she just sat there, thinking and worrying.

Dick, one of the houseboys who worked for another
family in the house, looked towards her and looked away
again without speaking. Most young Nigerian men spent a
year or two as houseboys. They worked for their unmarried
cousins or uncles and went to night school, while their male
relations saved up the bride price for their future wives.
Aku-nna's own father had been a houseboy too. Usually
Dick laughed at Aku-nna, but today he seemed kind and
sympathetic. She wondered why.

Suddenly she heard a shout. 'Aku-nna . . . oooo!' It was Aunt Uzo.

'Yes, Auntie!' Aku-nna called, jumping up and looking in the direction of the shout. Aunt Uzo came nearer and greeted her quietly.

'I'm glad I've found you at last,' she said. She looked tired. In her arms she carried a big, strong baby boy. Aku-nna saw the baby and smiled, and Uzo smiled too.

When she smiled the tiredness left Uzo's face for a moment and she looked young and carefree again. Then her old tired look returned. But Aunt Uzo was not an old woman. This baby was her first one, and he was eighteen months old. Uzo was probably only about nineteen years old, but her fat, greedy baby seemed to tire her out.

Uzo was a famous storyteller who knew hundreds of wonderful stories. 'Tonight I will tell you a new story,' she said. 'Hurry and do your cooking now.' As Aku-nna hesitated, Uzo spoke sharply. 'You heard me, girl – now hurry!'

'Why is it so urgent?' Aku-nna wondered. 'And what is so different about today?' She looked at Uzo's face, but found no answer there.

She went to the kitchen and tried to light her stove. But the wood would not burn. She knelt down and blew and blew. The smoke blew into her eyes and nose. Around her in the smoke-filled kitchen other people were busy with their cooking. Normally they sang and talked. Today they seemed unusually quiet.

Dick was cooking at the stove next to Aku-nna. He looked at her kindly. 'Your wood isn't dry enough,' he said.

'Here, move your pot onto my stove. I've finished now.'

Aku-nna was very surprised. Dick had never been so kind to her before. She started to cook yams for herself and her brother.

Soon she had finished. Her eyes were red and sore from the smoke and her chest felt tight and painful. She stood up and walked out of the kitchen with her pot on her head. On her way back to their apartment she looked for her brother, but without success.

She entered the apartment and found Uzo there, without her baby. Uzo looked troubled, and Aku-nna noticed for the first time that her eyes were red and swollen. She wanted to ask why, but that would not be respectful. Uzo spoke sharply to Aku-nna.

'Hurry and eat your share of the supper. Your brother will come home when he's hungry. Don't wait for him.'

Aku-nna obeyed, while Uzo stared emptily out of the window. Then there was a loud knock at the door and Aunt Mary appeared, holding Nna-nndo by the hand. She too looked very unhappy.

Suddenly Aku-nna understood the reason for the sudden visitors, their red, swollen eyes and the uncomfortable silences.

'Father is dead,' she thought. But at the same time the whole idea seemed unreal. 'This isn't happening to me,' thought Aku-nna. 'It's just a dream. Soon I shall wake up and Father will be here.'

Then her brother's high, childish voice broke the silence. 'We have no father,' he said.

'But Nna-nndo, you are wrong,' thought Aku-nna. 'It's

11

worse than that. We have nothing. Our father named you Nna-nndo, "Father is the shelter". We have not only lost our father. We have lost our shelter too.'

It has always been like that in Nigeria. When you have lost your father, you have lost everything. Your mother is only a woman; she cannot do anything for you. A fatherless family is a family without a head, a family without a home.

3

The Funeral

Most ceremonies in Nigeria combine European customs with native ones. Ezekiel Odia himself was a Christian and a church-goer, but he always called in a native medicine man when he wanted one. Ezekiel's funeral was like that too, with both native and Christian ceremonies.

In Nigeria mourning is an art. You do not just cry; you shout and sing about all the good things the dead person did in his lifetime. Some people are such good mourners that they are paid to mourn for complete strangers.

As soon as family and friends in Lagos heard of Ezekiel's death, the mourning began. Aku-nna and Nna-nndo were the chief mourners. They were expected to cry particularly loudly and desperately; after all, it was **their** father who had died. Aku-nna had seen her mother cry at the deaths of relations, so she knew what to do. She sang about her father.

'My father was a good provider. My father went to church every Sunday. He was a good husband to my mother, Ma Blackie. He bought me many dresses. He was kind to me. He sent me to school.' This was followed by a long, wordless cry of sadness. Then she sang, 'Who will be kind to me now? Who will send me to school? Who will feed me? Who will be a good husband to my mother? . . . Mother, come back from Ibuza! You have lost your husband. He married you according to local custom, and then again in the Christian church. And now he has gone. Come back, Mother! You have lost the father of your children . . .'

Aku-nna did not stop, even when the other mourners became tired. This was expected of a daughter. 'She is doing very well,' the neighbours said to each other.

Nna-nndo did not use many words, but screamed and threw himself about. The men held him so that he did not hurt himself. He soon stopped crying, but Aku-nna was encouraged to continue. It was right for girls to cry more than boys.

By this time the room was full of people. They poured in from all over Lagos. Each new arrival looked at the two children, listened for a moment to Aku-nna's crying, then went out onto the veranda and started to cry too. They all knew that death would come to everyone. So they did not cry only for Ezekiel and his children. They cried for themselves too.

Gradually, the mourners became tired. The first part of their mourning was almost over, and one by one the men went out into the open air. The near-relations of the dead man remained inside the house, crying and singing.

13

The moon was full and bright. It was a hot night and the men took off their shirts. They joined hands in a big circle and began to move from side to side, wordlessly. Then a voice rang out. The singer was calling on Death.

'Wake up, Death, and see what you have done! You took Nna-nndo's father away from him! You took Ezekiel away before he could enjoy the bride price from his daughter Akunna. You took him away for ever and ever!'

Now the men began to dance – still in a circle, hand in hand. Round and round they went, faster and faster, kicking up clouds of dust, singing loudly and wildly. The women came out to join their men. Soon the circle became too large and broke up into several smaller ones.The men's job was done. They had called Death from sleep. Now it was the turn of the women to sing for Ezekiel on his last, lonely journey. Each woman had a gourd with small stones inside. As they danced and sang, they shook the gourds and the stones inside sounded like raindrops on a roof.

Then the Christian songs began. They mixed with the noise of the gourds and the death songs and the crying of the mourners inside the house, in one storm of sound. Then, gradually, the mourners became tired, and the singing and dancing and crying stopped. Cool native wine and plates of nuts were handed round. Tired mourners slept on the ground.

The moon disappeared. The grey morning mist was everywhere; then the sun rose, and a new day began.

Indoors, Aku-nna had not slept much. There were too many people, and some of them were noisy sleepers. At last she got up carefully from between the sleeping bodies.

'Who will be kind to me now? Who will send me to school? Who will feed me?' sang Aku-nna.

One of her uncles was asleep across the doorway of the room. He woke and greeted Aku-nna sleepily. When Aku-nna tried to return the greeting, she discovered that she had lost her voice. 'How will I be able to cry at Father's funeral now?' she thought.

She went to the big water pot. Every family had one, and it was Aku-nna's job to fill theirs for her family every evening, so that her father could wash himself in the morning before leaving for work. Aku-nna knew that she had not filled the pot because of all the events of the evening before. But when she lifted the tin cover, she was surprised to find it full of cool water.

'Who did this?' she wondered. 'Perhaps one of the neighbours did it.'

Then suddenly the realization of her father's death hit her. 'I shall never see my father alive again,' she thought. 'His death has changed my whole life.' She wanted to cry aloud, but she had no voice. Her whole body felt heavy with sadness. But she used some water from the pot to wash her face and mouth. Its coolness made her feel a little better. She walked back to the apartment. Then she heard a voice calling her name.

'Aku-nna, oooo!'

She set out in the direction of the voice. She could not answer; her throat was still too sore. Her chest felt heavy. She pulled at her thin shirt.

'Aku-nna!' said Uzo crossly. 'You'll tear your shirt! You have no father now, to buy you new clothes. Nobody will buy you any until you marry. Then your husband will take care of you.'

16

'Ah well,' said another woman, 'they'll marry her off quickly. Then her bride price will pay for Nna-nndo's education.'

'That won't be difficult,' said Uzo. 'She's not ugly, and she's nice and quiet and intelligent. Any educated man will be glad to pay a good price for her.'

'Is that supposed to make me feel better?' thought Aku-nna. Her fear of the unknown future grew and grew.

The sun climbed in the sky and the food-sellers were out in the street, carrying their pots of hot foot on their heads.

'What do you want for breakfast this morning?' asked Uzo.

'I'm not hungry, thank you,' replied Aku-nna. 'Where is Nna-nndo?'

'He's with Mama John. He'll be all right. Come on, let's get some bananas for your sore throat. Mine is sore too, after all that crying.'

The rest of the day was like a bad dream. People came and went. They sang and danced and cried. Nna-nndo and Aku-nna sat quietly among all the noise and the comings and goings.

'I wish the children's mother was here,' someone said. 'They look so lost.'

They felt lost too. Suddenly there was a loud noise outside the house, and for a moment the noise inside the house stopped. The dancers stopped dancing, the Christians stopped singing. Everyone began to shout and scream.

'Cry now,' shouted Uzo to Aku-nna. 'Cry. Your father went into hospital a few weeks ago, and now he has come back! He has come to say his last goodbye.'

Then the children understood. Their father's body had been brought home. Aku-nna and her brother were taken to a neighbour's apartment, where they waited until Ezekiel's body was ready to see. Then they were called to pay their last respects to their father in his narrow wooden box.

Uncle Uche pointed to little Nna-nndo. 'Look,' he shouted to the other mourners. 'Our brother is lying here now, but he is not dead. He has left a son behind him. One day we shall all be proud of Nna-nndo . . .'

The time soon came to close the box. Aku-nna looked down at her father's body. 'How small he looks,' she thought, 'and how different, in his best suit.' She threw herself down in a storm of crying. Then the box was closed for ever.

Akinwunmi Street in Lagos had never seen such a long line of mourners on their way to the graveyard. The factory had sent their own special funeral car, with NIGERIAN ENGINE FACTORY painted on the side in gold. Ezekiel's friends from work laid him in the car. Nna-nndo and his sister followed the car, and after them came the singers from the Christian church. Hundreds of friends and neighbours followed, together with anyone else who felt like joining the group. Last of all came the mourners with their death songs and dances, their hand-clapping and their stone-filled gourds. A horn-blower was there too, blowing and blowing until his face was red. Other men had empty bottles and tin teaspoons. They knocked the spoons against the bottles as they walked along.

Ezekiel's body was lowered into the grave. Nobody cried any more. Aku-nna watched her brother pouring a handful of sand into the grave. Automatically, wordlessly, she did the same. Then all the other mourners began pouring sand, soil, stones, anything they could find, over her father's body. She wanted to call to them, to beg them to be gentle. Then she realized how silly that was. Her father was dead. He could not feel it.

The gravediggers were impatient to finish the job. The sound of the soil hitting the box was like a final goodbye to the children.

'Always remember that you are mine,' their father had said. Aku-nna took her brother's hand and they walked together out of the graveyard.

4

The Journey to Ibuza

The journey from Lagos to Ibuza is like a bridge between two different worlds. Lagos is a very busy port, the old capital of Nigeria. But it is above all a town of the Yoruba people. Ibuza, on the other hand, is a small town of the Ibo people, and it lies near the great river Niger that gives Nigeria its name.

Several weeks had passed since the funeral of Ezekiel Odia. His wife, Ma Blackie, had returned to Lagos from Ibuza to find her husband already dead and buried. Friends and relations were very kind to her and the two children, but life in Lagos was too expensive for a fatherless family.

*The bus carrying them to Ibuza drove through thick
and mysterious forests.*

So Ma Blackie and her children had to return to their home town, Ibuza, where Okonkwo, Ezekiel Odia's elder brother, and his family lived.

The children were sad to leave Lagos. It was the only home they had ever known, and Aku-nna wondered very much what their new life would be like. As the bus carrying them to Ibuza drove out of Lagos, she stared out of the windows, thinking and worrying. She knew only that she would have to marry, and that her bride price would help to educate her brother Nna-nndo. She did not mind that too much, but she wondered what her husband would be like. She hoped she would not have to marry a farmer, as she had heard how hard farm life could be for a woman. But there was nothing she could do about it, except ask God to help them all.

The bus hurried through many little Yoruba towns. After it passed Benin, the countryside changed. The soil was redder and the forests were thicker and more mysterious. The women were tall and beautiful and carried themselves proudly.

Ma Blackie and the children slept a little during the night, and before sunrise next morning they reached Asaba, which was the nearest town to Ibuza. The bus stopped in the market place near the river, and the children were woken by the voice of a food-seller. 'Buy my tasty rice! You'll love it!'

Nna-nndo woke Ma. 'We're hungry, Ma,' he insisted.

But Ma was cross. 'You haven't washed your face, son. Aku-nna, take your brother to the river. You must both wash your faces and hands. Our relations will be here at sunrise, because today is market day. I don't want them to

21

see you both looking dirty. Take this pot and bring me some water too, so that I can wash my face.'

'But I want some rice now, Ma,' begged Nna-nndo.

'No wash, no rice, do you hear me? Nice people wash before they eat. Go and wash your face.'

Nna-nndo was ashamed. He followed his sister obediently, looking back longingly at the rice-seller.

The sun rose, warm and golden. Ma Blackie and the children all enjoyed their rice, and little hot cakes too. While they ate, their bags were unloaded from the bus.

'Soon our people will come,' said Ma. 'And they will take us to Ibuza.'

'Is it far to Ibuza?' asked Aku-nna.

'Only seven miles. We shall be home soon. Ah, look! Here they come. They've seen us!'

She pointed to a group of about fifteen women who were coming towards them. Each was carrying a big basket of cassava on her head. Ma Blackie called out to them and they hurried to welcome the Odia family. They were kind and sympathetic.

'We'll sell our cassava quickly in the market,' they told Ma. 'Then we'll help you to carry your luggage to Ibuza.'

And in less than half an hour the women were back. They shared the family's bags and boxes between them, and they all walked together towards Ibuza, talking cheerfully all the way.

A big, loud-voiced girl called Ogugua carried Aku-nna's school books on her head. 'I'm sure we shall be friends,' said Ogugua. Ezekiel's elder brother Okonkwo was her father, so she was Aku-nna's cousin. 'You know,' she said, 'we

22

were both born in the same week – you in Lagos, I in Ibuza. I've heard so many nice things about you. We'll be like sisters – especially if your mother comes to live with my father.'

'Why should my mother live with your father?' asked Aku-nna, puzzled.

Ogugua laughed. 'You're almost fourteen and you still don't know our customs! Your mother will become my father's wife. My father has inherited everything your father owned, and he has "inherited" your mother too.'

'Oh dear!' cried Aku-nna.

'Don't worry, cousin. We shall all live happily together. Look – you see that woman over there?' She pointed to a tall, thin woman in front, who was carrying Ma Blackie's cooking pots on her head.

'What about her?' asked Aku-nna.

'Well, her husband was a big man in a white man's job somewhere in Northern Nigeria. Three years ago he died suddenly.'

'How terrible!' said Aku-nna.

'Yes,' agreed her cousin. 'Well, they'd been married for ten years, and they only had one daughter.'

'How terrible!' said Aku-nna again.

'But listen,' said Ogugua excitedly. 'That woman was inherited by her husband's brother. He is a chief – an *obi*. He has other wives, of course, so she's not his first wife, but she's very happy. And now she has a son!'

'Wonderful!' cried Aku-nna, clapping her hands. 'It's just like a story in a book.'

They were a long way behind the others now, and Ma

Blackie turned and called out to them to hurry up. Suddenly Aku-nna looked at her mother like a stranger. She realized how tall and straight and handsome Ma Blackie was. 'Poor Ma,' she thought, 'She's never had to work in the fields or carry heavy baskets. I hope her new husband is kind to her.' She thought about her own education. Her father had talked of sending her to college, but there was no hope of that now. 'I hope my new father will let me stay at school and get my certificate,' she thought. But there was nothing she could do about that.

The women had started talking again and Ogugua was listening to every word. But Aku-nna walked along deep in thought.

Suddenly they heard a bicycle bell behind them. The rider, a young man of perhaps eighteen or nineteen, was very tall and thin, with a pointed chin. He was a teacher at the church school in Ibuza, where Aku-nna and Nna-nndo would be going. He knew Ma Blackie and had heard of Ezekiel's death, so he greeted her warmly.

'Children,' said Ma, 'this is your new teacher.'

'Good morning, sir,' said Aku-nna and Nna-nndo shyly. The teacher looked kindly at Aku-nna. She felt shy, and looked down at the ground. He talked cheerfully for a while, then rode off towards Ibuza.

They walked past the Ibuza farms with their yam and cassava plants, and they met men on their way to the fields. When they reached the little Atakpo stream, they rested on its bank.

'Come and have a swim,' said Ogugua to Aku-nna.

'With all these people watching?' said Aku-nna, shocked.

24

'Don't be shy, cousin. What are you hiding?'

'Some men might see me,' said Aku-nna. 'What if that teacher is still somewhere around? He might see me.'

Her cousin laughed. 'What if he does? Why should your body be more interesting than all the others? And anyway, he's had lots of girlfriends.'

Ogugua swam away from her cousin. She was not pleased. She had seen the teacher staring at Aku-nna and she was a little jealous. She swam back to the bank, where Aku-nna was sitting with her tired feet in the cool water.

'You must take care,' Ogugua said. 'Don't get too friendly with that teacher. He's not one of us. No nice girl from a good family is allowed to talk to him.'

'Why? What do you mean?' asked Aku-nna. But Ogugua swam away again without answering.

They arrived in the village by mid-morning. Okonkwo was waiting, and when he saw them in the distance, he took off his good clothes and put on old, dirty ones. Then he sat down on the floor and began to cry loudly. Other people heard him and came to join in. It became a day of mourning for Okonkwo's brother, Ezekiel Odia.

'Who married his wife in church?' they sang. 'Who bought rich gifts for his children? Who was a good provider?' On and on they went.

'How strange,' thought Aku-nna. 'Five minutes ago the women were all discussing the latest fashions.' When even Ogugua began to cry, she had to do the same. 'If this is how they behave in Ibuza,' she thought, 'I'd better do the same. After all, I'm going to be one of them.'

The young men of the village started to build a special mourning hut for Ma Blackie, and in less than two hours they had finished. She had to stay there for nine full moons and mourn for her dead husband. During that time she was not allowed to leave her hut, or have a bath, or cut or comb her hair. And the women had prepared an old, torn dress for her to wear.

However, Ma Blackie had arrived in a new black cotton dress, which caused some argument among the women. Some said that Ma Blackie could wear her new dress during her mourning time. Others said she must wear the old one.

It was Okonkwo who decided. He was the head of the family, and he planned to become a chief as soon as he could get enough money together. He had already inherited his brother's wife and everything his brother owned, and now he was looking forward to getting a good bride price for his brother's daughter.

'Let Ma Blackie wear her new dress if she wants to,' he said kindly. 'It's bad enough that she's a widow. Why must she be dirty as well?'

Okonkwo's three wives all understood the message behind his words. Okonkwo wanted his dead brother's widow to stay in the family, to be his fourth wife.

5

Traditions

I buza was on the western side of the River Niger. Its inhabitants were Ibos and followed all the Ibo traditions. Even those who left their village to work in the white men's world took their traditions with them. According to these traditions, Ma Blackie spent nine months in her special mourning hut. Then a new hut was built for her and she became Okonkwo's fourth wife.

Ma earned a little money by clever buying and selling. With Ezekiel's savings she bought oil. She sold it to the white man, who took it back to England and made it into soap. Then she bought the white man's soap and sold it to her people.

As the months passed, she became prouder than ever of her children. Aku-nna was now almost fifteen. She was an intelligent girl, with the promise of beauty in her large, gentle eyes and smooth skin. Nna-nndo too was growing fast and doing well. The fact that both children were at school caused some jealousy in Okonkwo's family. The other wives did not mind too much about Nna-nndo. After all, he was a boy. Also, in his lifetime Ezekiel had paid a few shillings every week to the Church Friendly Society. This meant that after his death the Society paid for his son's education up to the age of fifteen. So nobody, not even Okonkwo, could take Nna-nndo away from school.

'How clever of my brother,' thought Okonkwo, 'to

provide for his son in this way. Why didn't I think of that for my sons?'

But Okonkwo's sons, Iloba and Osenekwu, had no use for book-learning.

'School,' they said, 'is no use to a free man. School is a place to send your slaves.'

That was another tradition. In the old days, when the white men first started their Christian schools, the local free men had no use for them. They sent their slaves to school to please the white men, while their own free-born sons stayed at home and followed the old traditions. Later events showed, however, that it was these educated slaves who got the top jobs. The sons and grandsons of these 'slave' families were now so rich and powerful that they seemed to command the respect of everyone.

'Why do you let your brother's children go to school?' demanded Okonkwo's eldest son, Iloba. He was twenty years old, and was a farmer, working hard to buy himself a wife.

'The Friendly Society pays for Nna-nndo,' said his father.

'Very well. But the girl – Aku-nna – why waste money on her?'

'It's not my money that is wasted,' answered Okonkwo. 'Her mother pays for her education. And Aku-nna won't be going to college. She has only a few more months of school.' He laughed loudly. His sons looked puzzled. 'You don't understand,' said Okonkwo. 'Don't you know that I hope to become a chief, an *Obi*?'

To become an *Obi* a man had to offer a large, expensive gift to the gods. Then he received the red hat which was the

28

'Aku-nna's bride price will come to me,' said Okonkwo.

29

mark of a chief, and there were days of celebration. Indeed, in the old days a slave was put to death to celebrate this great event. It all cost a great deal of money.

'Well, what has that to do with Aku-nna?' Iloba asked.

'Aku-nna and your sister Ogugua will get married at about the same time. Their bride prices will come to me, and these days, people pay more for educated girls.'

Now his sons understood. 'So Aku-nna's name will come true,' they thought. 'She will truly become a "father's wealth". Unfortunately, her own father did not live to enjoy this wealth. But not to worry – Okonkwo is almost a father to her now.' They smiled at their father's cleverness. 'He needed money in order to become an *Obi*,' they thought. 'Aku-nna's bride price will provide that money. She will marry a rich man, and make us rich too.'

They walked silently to the hut of their mother, Ngbeke, who was Okonkwo's first wife. At the door Iloba said, 'It's happening everywhere these days. Didn't you hear, the local doctor is getting married to a girl whose parents are asking for two hundred pounds for her.'

'Two hundred pounds? What's so special about her?' demanded Osenekwu.

'She's a hospital nurse. That's all. People who've seen her say that she's not particularly beautiful. But they say the doctor loves her.'

'Perhaps, but that is a lot of money to pay for an ordinary woman,' his brother answered. He thought for a moment and added, 'I hope we get plenty of money for Aku-nna.'

They both laughed as they bent their tall bodies to go through the low doorway into their mother's hut.

Ngbeke looked at her sons sharply. 'What have you two and your father been talking about?' she demanded.

'It is talk between men,' replied seventeen-year-old Osenekwu importantly. 'Ogugua, our sister, please bring our food!'

'Ogugua is filling my pipe for me,' their mother said shortly.

In fact, Ogugua was doing nothing. She was sitting combing her hair and listening to every word. She took the big pipe and began to fill it. She lit it with a burning stick from the fire and handed it to her mother. Ngbeke took a big mouthful of smoke before she spoke again.

'So my sons are so grown up that I can no longer share their thoughts?' she demanded. She laughed bitterly, showing her black teeth, which were the result of years of smoking. 'Well, I will tell **you** something. I am Okonkwo's first wife, and I say that he's making a big mistake. He's wrong to expect so much from his brother's daughter.'

Iloba cried, 'But Mother, Aku-nna is like a daughter to him now. In fact, according to our law and tradition she **is** his daughter now.'

'Be quiet and eat your yams, my son,' replied his mother. 'You know nothing.'

'Aku-nna is going to marry a rich man,' said Osenekwu. 'She'll make us all rich.'

'Be quiet!' said his mother. 'What rich man is she going to marry? The son of a slave, who teaches at her school? Can you be sure that her mother will not keep the bride price for herself? You forget that her mother was married in the church. She was educated by the white men and she

31

knows their laws. Oh, you forget many things, my sons.'

Ngbeke's sons did not understand. What was she talking about? Surely Ma Blackie was not taking advantage of their father, just to educate her own children?

Iloba shouted, 'My father will have that bride price! No one else can use the money!'

'What about Nna-nndo?' said his mother. 'A few days ago Ma Blackie told me that she wanted him to go to college. How will she pay for that? The white man's law will be on her side if she demands her daughter's bride price to pay for her son's education. So you had better tell your father to stop dreaming about bride prices. Who will want her anyway? She'll never have children; she's too small and thin. And she's not even a woman yet! Look at your sister – she's the same age, and she's a real woman. You could marry her off tomorrow! That Aku-nna will come to no good, I tell you. She and her mother are too proud.'

Ngbeke's sons stared. They did not see the jealousy in their mother's eyes. 'She could be right,' they thought. 'It's true. Aku-nna is different. She's not allowed to play rough games in the moonlight, or to join in the dancing at Christmas. She's too soft and quiet. And that teacher is always lending her books! Yes, perhaps Mother is right. Here she is, nearly fifteen, still at school and not yet ready for marriage. What kind of girl is that?'

'Mother,' said Iloba aloud, 'do you think she might be an *ogbanje*, a "living dead"?'

His mother was glad. Her sons had not noticed her jealousy. Ngbeke did not like Ma Blackie and was very jealous of her. She did not mind Okonkwo's two younger wives, because they respected and obeyed her. But Ma Blackie was handsome and intelligent and proud. However, Ngbeke had to hide her true feelings from her sons.

'Yes, I'm sure Aku-nna is an *ogbanje*,' she said. 'She's too quiet. I must speak to her mother about it tomorrow. An *ogbanje* doesn't belong in this world. They all die young, usually at the birth of their first child. They have to die young, because their friends in the other world call them back. I'm glad that none of my daughters is an *ogbanje*.'

'Can't we save her, Mother?' asked Iloba. He was frightened now. Although he was only twenty, he had seen many young girls die in childbirth. Their deaths were always very painful, and he did not want his little cousin Aku-nna to die like that.

'Perhaps,' said Ngbeke, 'if you have a good medicine man. It all costs a lot of money. That is what her mother should be doing. And she should certainly not let Aku-nna talk to the son of Ofulue!'

'Chike Ofulue?' cried Iloba in horror. 'The school teacher? But he's the son of slaves, Mother, and he knows it. Chike is only Aku-nna's teacher. She has to talk to him, because she's his student. But she can't be interested in him, she really can't!'

'If she is, I will kill her,' said Osenekwu softly.

All this time Ogugua had been listening quietly. Aku-nna was her friend, as well as her cousin. She could not accuse her mother of jealousy; that was not respectful. But she did her best.

'Chike likes Aku-nna,' she said, 'But that's only because she's eager to learn and he wants to help her. He knows he's

33

from a slave family. He was born here and knows our customs. He's sure to marry a girl from another slave family, not the daughter of a free family from Ibuza. Brothers, there's no need to worry.'

'There is no smoke without fire, my children,' said Ngbeke.

'It's just talk, Mother,' said Ogugua. 'How could a quiet girl like that interest a clever man like Chike, a teacher – and a slave?'

'Perhaps you're right,' said her mother. 'But don't forget that Chike's family have money. And money buys a lot these days . . .'

'No smoke without fire,' Ngbeke had said, and she was right. Chike Ofulue was falling in love with his fifteen-year-old student. He was helpless to stop himself. He had never seen a girl so unsure of herself, so afraid of her own people.

The school in Ibuza where Chike taught was a church as well. It was a long, white building, with round windows and a roof covered in leaves.

When they had started coming to this school a year ago, the first thing that Aku-nna and her brother had noticed was the size of the boys. Most of them were young men. There were only three girls in the whole school, and Aku-nna was the oldest of them. On that first day she had felt very lost and shy, and had almost jumped when she heard a voice saying 'hello' behind her.

She had turned to find the teacher behind her, and had said, shyly, 'Good morning, sir.'

'What do you think of our school?' he had asked her. 'I

'*What do you think of our school?*' *Chike asked Aku-nna.*

expect it seems very different from your school in Lagos.'

He was right, but she had been too shy to answer. She just smiled politely.

Before school began on that first day, there had been a short service. Afterwards, the white man in the white suit, who was in charge of the church, spoke to them all. His name was Father Osborne, and he came from England. But he was certainly not speaking English. Then Aku-nna caught a few words, and she realized that this big, kind man with the sun-burned face was trying to speak Ibo, her own language. He welcomed them all to school after the holidays and hoped they would all work hard. He hoped all their families were well. 'Please give my personal greetings and best wishes to everyone,' he said. The whole school clapped and cheered. Father Osborne's Ibo was a little odd, but he had said the right thing, after all.

After a year, Aku-nna and Nna-nndo had become used to Ibuza. At school they learned the white man's ways. Then they came home to the countless, unchanging traditions of their own people. They were trapped, like two helpless little fish, between the two sets of traditions.

One thing Aku-nna knew for certain. Her mother no longer had any time for her: she was too busy with her business and her new husband. Aku-nna was a very unimportant member of a large and busy family. She was a quiet and lonely girl. But to Chike Ofulue she was becoming very special indeed.

6

The Slaves

'In the sight of God, we are all the same.' That was what Father Osborne said, and that was what all good Christians believed. But in the eyes of his own people Chike still belonged to a family who had once been slaves, and no free man would allow a slave to marry his daughter.

None of this worried Chike much. He was handsome, and the local girls pretended not to know that he was from a slave family. After all, his family had produced many rich and successful men. In fact, he looked down on the local girls. They were not good enough for an educated man like him. He enjoyed himself with them, but he did not respect them.

Chike's parents knew about his adventures with local girls, but did not try to stop him. He had the money and the freedom to choose his own pleasures. So Chike was surprised when one day his father called him into his sitting-room for a talk.

It was a big, comfortable room with leather armchairs and a lot of family photographs on the walls. Chike's father, Ofulue, had been a teacher too. He had four wives, all from nearby towns, and he had enjoyed a comfortable, successful life. The people of Ibuza never forgave him for this and never, for example, allowed him to become a chief.

'When the son of a slave becomes a chief,' the free men said, 'then we know that the end is near!'

Ofulue was amused by it all. He did not want the people of Ibuza to do anything for him. He was a wealthy man and his children had important jobs in the schools and the hospitals.

Now Ofulue spoke seriously to Chike.

'I knew Aku-nna's father well. I would not like a son of mine to bring shame on his daughter. I saw the way you were looking at her in church. Everybody noticed it. I beg you not to harm that girl.'

Chike was surprised. He thought that he had succeeded in hiding his feelings. He said: 'I care for her. She is so alone. But I could never harm her.'

Ofulue looked hard at his son. 'You will have to study hard if you want to get to university this year.'

Chike felt angry. 'How could my father say such a hurtful thing?' he thought. 'He knows perfectly well that I passed all my examinations, but they still did not give me a scholarship.' That had hurt Chike terribly at the time. He still felt upset about it – why was his father reminding him now?

'Clearly they did not think I was good enough for a scholarship,' he said bitterly.

'Perhaps it's because you want to study sociology,' said his father. 'Perhaps the examiners have never heard of it. What can you do with a sociology degree? Can't you study something different, like law?'

Chike stared at the photographs on the walls. Each showed a successful member of the Ofulue family. 'So he wants me to be a doctor, or a lawyer or an engineer,' he thought. 'It's OK to talk about "my son the doctor", or "my son the lawyer", or "my son the engineer". But who can talk proudly of "my son the sociologist"?'

He said aloud, 'I don't want to change, Father. Sociology is very useful.'

'Then try again this year. Don't worry if they don't give you a scholarship. I'll pay for you to go away to university.'

Chike was beginning to understand. 'So Father wants me to leave Ibuza,' he thought.

Ofulue had never paid for higher education for any of his children, simply because there were too many of them. To be fair to all his wives, he had given every child the chance to take School Certificate. After that, each child was on his – or her – own. Girls were not particularly encouraged, but no one said no to them – if they won a scholarship. No scholarship, no education. Obviously Ofulue was very worried about Chike's relationship with Aku-nna, if he was willing to send Chike to university without a scholarship. Chike felt angry again.

'Surely she must be married one day?' he demanded.

His father looked at him very hard. 'Yes, of course – but not to you. You will leave that girl alone!' he said sharply. 'Now go!'

Chike did not sleep at all that night.

They say that forbidden fruit tastes sweet. Because Aku-nna was forbidden, Chike wanted her more than ever. Aku-nna too had been warned about Chike, but she did not understand what her family was warning her against. She did not know the history of 'slave' families. Although, under the white man's law, nobody could own a person as a slave now, people did not forget which families had been slaves in the old days. But nobody had explained to Aku-nna what it meant to be from a 'slave' or a 'free' family.

Chike tried hard to prepare his students for their examinations. The day after his meeting with his father, he spoke to Aku-nna as little as possible. But that day Aku-nna seemed slow and stupid, and could not answer any of Chike's questions. In the end he became angry.

'What's the matter with you, Aku-nna?' he demanded. 'Didn't you do your homework?'

'She didn't have time,' said a boy behind her. 'She was with her boyfriends.' The boys all laughed. Aku-nna burst into tears and the boys laughed louder than ever.

'Who said that?' Chike asked angrily. A boy stood up. 'You should be ashamed of yourself,' said Chike. All the boys looked uncomfortable. 'Aku-nna, you may go,' said Chike gently. 'Now, everyone – open your books at page eleven.'

Aku-nna rushed blindly out of the room. What was the matter with her? She did not know. She sat down heavily under a big orange tree at the end of the school field, and cried and cried. Tears poured down her face like rain water. She let them flow. It was quiet and private under the orange tree. She watched two little birds feeding their babies. They looked so happy together. 'I am alone,' she thought. 'There is nobody I can talk to.'

In the distance the school bell rang, but that was in another world. Aku-nna was alone in her private world of tears and loneliness.

'Aku-nna, you need your certificate, don't you?' said a gentle voice.

She looked up and saw Chike standing over her. 'If you fail your examination, your family won't let you take it again.'

Aku-nna could not answer. She just looked up at his anxious face, then down at his neat white shoes. Tears filled her eyes again. Chike sat down beside her under the orange tree. He said, 'I will help you to pass your examination before I leave this horrible place.'

'Leave? Where are you going?' The anxiety in her voice showed how much she cared.

'University,' he said. He took her hand, and rather roughly he pulled her to her feet.

As she stood up, she felt a pain in her back. Her legs felt weak and she felt strangely cold, although it was a warm day.

'Do you want me to go?' he asked.

She shook her head. She did not want to seem badly brought up. So how could she tell him how she felt about him? Tears filled her eyes again.

'Why are you so sad?' said Chike kindly. 'Why do you cry so much? I'd like to make you cry with happiness! Come now, we must go back to school.' Then he stopped, and looked sharply at Aku-nna. 'Child, you're bleeding! There's blood on your dress.'

She turned round quickly and saw the blood. At first she thought that she had hurt herself. Then she realized what was happening to her. She had heard the women talk about this bleeding. When they were bleeding like this, women

41

were 'unclean' and for those few days each month, there were a lot of things they were not allowed to do.

'So now I am a woman too,' she thought. 'I can be married. Any man can cut a piece of my hair, and carry me away.' That was the tradition. That piece of hair made the girl his, for ever.

Suddenly the pain became more violent, and she felt deeply ashamed. She wanted to run away from Chike. How could she let him see her like this?

Chike came nearer. He did not care if anyone saw them. He wanted to marry this girl, even if he had to break all the laws of his people. He held her tightly. 'Is this the first time?' he asked.

'Yes,' she whispered.

They stood there for a long time. Neither of them wanted to go. Then the pain came again.

'Sit down and wait here,' he said. 'I'll get you something.'

She obeyed. 'Of course, Chike knows all about such things,' she thought. 'He has sisters of his own, after all. But how can I keep my secret? If Okonkwo finds out about this, he will want me to marry at once, because he wants my bride price. But I want to stay at school and get my certificate. What can I do?'

Chike returned with a glass of water and two white tablets. He gave her his big wool jacket that he wore on cold mornings. Then, as she took the tablets, he said, 'Can you keep quiet about this? Don't tell anyone till after the exam.'

'How can I hide it?' she asked. 'I sleep in the same hut as my mother; she's sure to notice.'

'My brother is a doctor. I know what white women use.

Go home now. I'll tell your brother that you have a
headache. And please make sure that your dress is covered
by that jacket.' He added, 'I love you,' and walked away.

'I must hurry home,' thought Aku-nna, 'before anyone
sees me.' The tablets helped the pain in her back, but she still
felt very conscious of the blood on her dress.

Her mother's hut was a mile from the school. By the time
she got there, her head was aching and she felt sick. There
was a little water in the pot, and she washed herself with it.

'My brother will be angry when he comes home and finds
the pot empty,' she thought. But she felt too ill to care. She
lay down and fell into a troubled sleep.

'Aku-nna!' Her brother was calling. 'What's the matter
with you this time? You're always ill.' He went to the water
pot. It was a hot afternoon and he was thirsty. But the pot
was empty.

'This pot was almost full this morning. What's happened
to it?'

'Perhaps Ma drank it,' said Aku-nna.

'Liar! If you think I'm going to go to the stream just for
you, you're mistaken. What did you do with the water,
anyway?'

She did not reply, and he did not insist on an answer.
Then he went out to borrow some water from a neighbour.
Aku-nna was glad to see him go. She fell asleep again.

Later her cousin Ogugua came into the hut. 'What's the
matter? Have you forgotten that we promised to meet our
mothers and help them to carry their shopping home?'

'I'm not well,' said Aku-nna. 'Please carry some of my
mother's things for her.'

43

Ogugua filled a lamp with oil and lit it. In the soft yellow light she studied her cousin's face.

'It's a headache, isn't it? Your eyes are very red. Don't worry, I'll carry your mother's shopping for her.'

Aku-nna did not lie down again. 'Ma will be home soon,' she thought. Then she heard a gentle knock at the door.

It was Chike. He sat down beside her and put his arm around her.

'What shall we do?' he asked her.

'Tell my people that you want to marry me,' she whispered.

'How can I?' he demanded. 'Haven't you heard that my father is the son of a slave?'

'Don't say that,' said Aku-nna. 'There is no other person for me in this world, Chike . . .'

He started kissing her, the way the white men did in films. Aku-nna had read about kissing in *True Love Stories*. She found that she did not particularly enjoy it, but Chike obviously did. 'You will always be mine,' he whispered in her ear.

'What will he do next?' she thought anxiously. She stood up. 'My mother will be home soon,' she said.

Just then they heard voices outside the hut. Chike waited to welcome Ma Blackie and Nna-nndo home.

'Aku-nna felt ill in school,' he explained. 'So I came to see how she was. Look, I've brought her this bottle of headache tablets. I hope she'll be better soon.'

Ma Blackie said, 'She'll be back at school tomorrow.' She gave him a long, hard look that said, 'Be careful!'

'Good night,' said Chike. Ma Blackie answered, but Aku-nna did not. So many things had happened to her in one day, so many things that she did not understand.

7

One of the Girls

Aku-nna had at last begun to feel that she was an Ibuza girl, and she and the other girls of the same age did everything together, except one thing. Every market day at Asaba, Aku-nna met Chike. The two of them sat in a quiet place by the river, and talked. He was teaching her the latest songs from a book that he had ordered from Lagos. Once or twice he gave her a gentle kiss, but that was all. To him she was very special, and he did not want to harm her.

She was getting to know Chike better. Although he talked a lot in the schoolroom, he was often quiet with her. They sat and listened to the sound of the river and the song of the birds, and the music of their own hearts.

Although these meetings remained a secret, it was obvious to everyone that Chike Ofulue was uncontrollably in love. Again and again his father warned him. Chike politely told his father that he was not going away to university without Aku-nna. 'What do I want a degree for, anyway?' Chike said. 'It might get me a better job, but will it make me a happier person? I want Aku-nna, Father. There is no other girl in the world for me.'

'If you marry her,' said his father, 'her family will never

'*Every market day I throw Aku-nna's bananas into the river
and we sit and talk . . .*'

forgive us. Already they hate us because we are wealthy and successful.'

'Father, I'm sorry to cause you so much trouble. But I dream about this girl every night. We're so happy, every market day, when I've thrown her bananas into the river and we sit and talk . . .'

His father smiled. 'And who pays for these bananas that you throw away, my son?'

'I do, Father. They don't cost much – only three shillings. She buys them for one shilling and sixpence, then she has to sell them in the market for three shillings. I buy them, then we throw them in the river and we have the rest of the day for ourselves. It's my only chance of talking to her. Her hut is always full of people.'

'Son, I must ask you one thing. Do not harm this girl! All girls must be virgins when they go to their husbands.'

'Father, nobody must have her except me.'

'And you must not kidnap her either. I know my mother was a slave, but I know how to behave. Tell me when she is ready to be married, and I'll visit her family and ask for her in the proper way.'

'And if they refuse, Father, what can we do?'

'We'll cross that bridge when we come to it. We can't do anything until she's a woman. Keep your eyes and ears open, and be ready to ask for her as soon as she's ready.'

The next day Chike told Aku-nna about this conversation with his father.

'Are your parents coming to ask for me in the proper way, then?' she asked.

'Yes,' he said.

She looked sadly at Chike. 'There will be trouble,' she said. The sun was setting and it was time for him to leave her. He held her tightly.

'I will come to your hut in three days' time,' he promised.

Three days later, on the afternoon of the day Chike was expected, Aku-nna and her friends all went out to look for firewood. There were about twelve of them and they felt safe and strong. Of course, they had no enemies, but in Ibuza an innocent young girl was not always safe. A man with no money to pay a bride price could hide behind the trees. He could jump out and cut a piece of hair from a girl's head. If he did that, she belonged to him for life and no other man could have her. That was why so many girls cut their hair very short . . . But there was safety in numbers.

When they reached the place where the firewood was, they hurried off in ones and twos. Aku-nna found a particularly big piece of wood. She pulled at it, but it would not come. She pulled harder, and the wood broke suddenly. She fell to the ground, scratching her hand. At that moment she felt a sharp pain in her back. This was the third time, and she knew what to expect. She still had not told her mother, but she knew she could not hide the blood from her friends this time.

Aku-nna sat on the ground and wondered what to do. She could not ask Chike; he was out fishing. 'Well,' she thought, 'I shall have to tell my mother – but it means I can be married off at any time.' She was afraid of the future and wished things could stay as they were.

48

As she sat there, she remembered another problem. According to native tradition, the river god did not allow unclean women in his river.

Just then she heard someone calling her name. Aku-nna stood up. Her back ached and she felt stiff all over. Ogugua's face appeared through the leaves.

'Aku-nna,' she whispered. 'What's the matter?'

Aku-nna told her, and Ogugua laughed and clapped her hands. She called to the others. 'Listen, girls!' cried Ogugua. 'We went out to fetch firewood with a girl, and we're coming home with a woman!'

Aku-nna felt mean and dishonest. After all, this was not really her first time.

The sun was going down as the girls walked home, singing and talking.

'Who are you going to marry?' the other girls asked Aku-nna. 'Has anyone asked for you yet?'

Aku-nna shook her head. But Ogugua laughed. 'Many men have asked for her,' she said, 'and my father told them that she was still only a child. But not any more!'

'Who has asked for her?' they demanded.

'The Nwanze family, and the Chigboes. And the Obidi family want her for their son, Okoboshi.'

Aku-nna had been at school with Okoboshi, and had not liked him at all. 'You say Okoboshi's father asked for me in marriage?' she said.

'Yes – and now lots more men will ask for you. You will fetch a big bride price, and everyone will be glad!'

Aku-nna was miserable. 'Surely Ma will not let me marry that horrible Okoboshi!' she thought. 'Ma promised me that

I could teach for a year or two before marrying. She will never let my uncle marry me off so soon.'

Aku-nna did not know everything, however. Ma Blackie was expecting Okonkwo's baby, and all she wanted was peace and quiet. She had no time for her daughter, and she could never refuse anything to the father of her baby. Aku-nna was alone, without the support of her mother.

The girls became quiet as they reached the stream. There was an old man there, with three old women. A long way along the bank Chike was quietly fishing. The other girls started to undress, but Aku-nna hesitated. The old man shouted to her.

'What's the matter? Don't be shy, dear!'

The old women guessed at once, and told him to be quiet. They called to Aku-nna. 'Come along, my dear. The river god will forgive you. He will know it is not your fault. And congratulations!'

Suddenly Aku-nna heard someone whistling. It was Chike. He had come nearer, and was whistling their favourite song.

'Brown skin girl, stay at home with the baby,

I have to go in my sailing boat . . .'

He turned away from her and concentrated on his fishing. But Aku-nna knew that he understood.

8

Kidnapped!

That evening was a time for celebration. Ma Blackie greeted her daughter with tears of happiness. Okonkwo was pleased too. Today was a very special day for him, and he ordered a party for Aku-nna.

'I'm glad I inherited Ma Blackie,' he thought. 'Now the girl's bride price will come to me. I wonder who will pay the highest price?'

Then he called to Aku-nna. 'Remember, Chike Ofulue is only a friend,' he said. 'Now that you're a woman, that friendship must die!'

'How can he behave like this?' thought Aku-nna. 'He's been in love, and knows what it's like. How can he forbid me to see the man I love?' But she knew the answer. He was not being unkind. He was simply obeying the laws of his people. Sadly she returned to her mother's hut.

Ma Blackie was sitting outside the hut with her friends. They were all laughing and talking loudly. 'Get ready,' she said to Aku-nna. 'Soon the young men will come to visit you.'

Aku-nna knew the custom. Now that she was a woman, the young men of the village were allowed to visit her. She took two headache tablets and put on her best skirt and her new pink shirt. Already she could hear the voice of her first visitor. It was the boy Okoboshi.

'May I come in?' he called.

'I'll kill myself if I have to marry him,' thought Aku-nna. Aloud she called, 'Just a moment.' Then she heard more voices. She came out of the hut to greet the young men. Each gave her a little present. She thanked them shyly, while they looked suspiciously at each other. Then they all went inside the hut, according to local tradition.

'Why hasn't Chike come?' wondered Aku-nna. 'Surely they can't prevent him from seeing me? Will those women outside the hut try to frighten him away?'

Then she heard Ma Blackie's voice outside the hut. 'Go in, then, but not for long. I shall be sending everyone away soon. I need my sleep, you know.'

Chike came into the hut. He greeted the other young men. Nobody answered, and before he could sit down beside Aku-nna, Okoboshi came forward.

'A free man can sit where he likes,' said Okoboshi. He sat down beside Aku-nna and put his hand inside her shirt. Aku-nna screamed, and Chike hit Okoboshi in the face. Aku-nna expected the others to attack Chike, but nobody moved.

Ma Blackie came rushing in to see what all the noise was about. She saw Okoboshi lying on the mud floor with his mouth covered with blood. She gave a little cry and turned to Chike.

'If you must fight, do it somewhere else!'

'Ma,' begged Aku-nna, 'don't be angry with Chike. Okoboshi was horrible. Look – he has torn my new shirt!'

'Don't be so shy and silly. How can he harm you with all those young men watching? I suppose you'd rather let a slave touch you!'

'How can Ma do this to me?' thought Aku-nna. 'I thought she liked Chike.' She burst into tears.

Then Chike was standing beside her. His nearness gave her strength. Friends and neighbours were loudly comforting Ma Blackie.

'Don't worry,' they were saying. 'She'll soon forget this slave, and marry a nice suitable boy. Now don't worry. Just concentrate on your new baby.'

That was another surprise for Aku-nna. So her mother was expecting Okonkwo's child! 'Now he has made her dreams come true,' thought Aku-nna. 'She won't be able to refuse him anything. If he wants to marry me off, she'll let him do it!'

At last the young men left and Aku-nna was able to go to bed. But she did not sleep much.

The next few days were quiet and nothing much happened. Then the night of the dance practice came. In Ibuza Christmas was an important time for everyone. The schools were closed and the teachers were on holiday. People who were working away from home came to celebrate Christmas with their families. Every Christmas, the fifteen-year-old girls did a special dance. The girls knew that for most of them it would be their last Christmas in their fathers' homes. So several times a week they practised the *aja* dance.

Aku-nna had not practised the dance with her friends in the beginning, because of her examinations. But now the examinations were over and all she could do was wait for the results. So now she joined in the dance practices.

Ogugua helped her, and Aku-nna began to enjoy the dancing very much.

The dance teacher was a tall, thin, proud old man called Zik, who was very good at making and singing the special *aja* songs. Aku-nna liked him.

This dance was the greatest moment in the girls' lives, and they knew it. 'When we are grandmothers,' said Ogugua, 'we shall take our pipes out of our toothless old mouths and we shall say to our grandchildren, "We did the best *aja* dance in the world!"'

That evening, Aku-nna and the other girls made their way to the dancing hut, carrying an oil lamp. This was one of Chike's presents to Aku-nna, and it was much better than a burning stick. As they crossed the wide sandy square in the middle of the village, they saw another light coming towards them. It was Chike, and they all greeted him cheerfully.

'I have some good news for you,' he said. 'But if I tell you now, you won't be able to concentrate on your dancing!'

They all begged him to tell them. 'Very well,' laughed Chike. 'Aku-nna has passed her examination. She can now be a teacher if she wants to.'

They clapped and shouted, then they questioned Chike about the boys.

He told them that Okoboshi had failed. 'I'm not surprised,' Chike added. 'He didn't do any work.'

'Okoboshi isn't a bad boy really,' said one of the girls. 'He's his mother's only son, and she lets him have everything he wants. It isn't his fault. Come on, or we'll be late for the dancing.'

They were late anyway, and Zik the dancing teacher was

'This is the end of all my dreams,' thought Aku-nna. 'They are kidnapping me.'

not pleased with them. He made them work harder than ever before.

'Come on, girls!' he shouted. 'Aku-nna, have you got a wooden leg? Bend your knees, child!' The girls practised hard for a long time.

Then suddenly the oil lamps in the dancing hut all went out. There was the sound of heavy feet. Strange voices, men's voices, were heard. At first the girls were too shocked to make a sound. Then they all began to scream at the tops of their voices. Some of them reached the door and tried to get out. But strong hands were holding the door closed. Then there were more footsteps, and strong hands caught Aku-nna around the waist.

'Here she is!' cried a voice. 'Let's go!'

Aku-nna tried to scream. But a rough hand covered her mouth and she was unable to make a sound.

'What's happening?' she thought. She could hear the dancing teacher's voice, shouting, demanding to know what was going on. Then she was carried on several strong shoulders. The door opened, and out they went.

Suddenly Aku-nna realized what was happening. 'This is the end of all my dreams,' she thought. 'They are kidnapping me.' She could not get away. There were at least twelve men, running, carrying her along. She lost consciousness, and she was still unconscious when she arrived at her new home.

9

A Forced Wedding

On his way home after meeting the girls, Chike thought about Aku-nna. 'How surprised and pleased she was when I told her about her examination results!' he said to himself. 'Her success will make things easier for both of us. I must make sure she gets the teaching job she wants. The money will be a big help to her mother and brother. And I shall have time to decide between the oil company and the university. Father has promised to talk to Okonkwo, but I must say he's taking his time about it. Perhaps he's been waiting for the results of Aku-nna's examination. And if Okonkwo will agree to the marriage, Father will gladly pay a hundred pounds. Father can easily afford it, and surely Okonkwo will be very glad to accept – it'll seem like a fortune to him.'

It was a very dark, moonless night. It was a night for murder, a night for fear. He stopped suddenly. He thought he heard someone calling his name. But when he lifted his lamp and looked around, he saw nothing except the black trees on each side of the path. The call came again. It was Aku-nna's voice. 'But that's impossible,' thought Chike. 'She's safe in the dancing hut with Zik and her friends. My imagination is playing tricks on me.' He walked faster, and his heart beat like a drum.

Then he heard a gun. It was followed by another shot, and another and another. Ibuza people always fired guns on their wedding night. He heard wedding music too, from the other side of the village.

'Why haven't I heard about this wedding?' thought Chike. 'Well, I expect my sisters will tell me all about it when I get home.'

He went straight to his father's house to tell him the good news about Aku-nna's examination.

'I'm glad, my son,' said Ofulue. 'And I have spoken to Okonkwo.'

'What did he say, Father?'

'He didn't say no, and he didn't say yes,' replied his father. 'We shall have to buy him. He wants to be a chief, and he'll use our money for that. But that means you will have to marry early, and I don't like that.'

'Oh, Father, Aku-nna is not sixteen yet. We can wait. She can take teacher training, or I can work with the oil company in Ughelli. I don't mind what we do. But I do want her to leave her uncle's family. They are not kind to her.'

'So I hear. I also heard that you knocked down Okoboshi a day or two ago.'

'Yes, I did. He was hurting Aku-nna. I had to stop him.'

Just then they heard more shots in the distance. The sounds of singing and dancing reached their ears.

'Who can be getting married on a night like this?' said Ofulue.

Suddenly Chike knew. He felt weak and sick. He almost fell to the floor. Holding tightly to the back of his father's big leather armchair, he whispered, 'I think that noise is coming from the Obidi family hut . . . I think they have kidnapped Aku-nna for their son Okoboshi.'

Moving forward, Ofulue laid a strong hand on his son's shoulder, and Chike cried like a child.

After their frightening experience in the dancing hut, the other girls ran home and told their parents what had happened.

'It was all so sudden – the lamps went out – somebody held the door shut – then the door was thrown open, and we all ran home.' It was a strange, confused story and their mothers decided to forget about it and let their men investigate it.

When they felt better, the girls told their mothers about Aku-nna's examination. Everyone was very pleased.

'Let's go and congratulate her family,' said Ngbeke, Okonkwo's first wife. So a small crowd arrived at Ma Blackie's hut.

'Please come in,' said Ma Blackie. 'My daughter is still dancing, and my son is out playing. But do come in.'

'Where did you say Aku-nna was?' said Ngbeke sharply.

'She went to the dancing.' Then Ma Blackie saw Ogugua and the other girls. 'I thought she was with you.'

Ngbeke suddenly realized what had happened, and shouted for her husband.

'Okonkwooooo! Wake up! They have kidnapped our daughter. Wake up, everyone, wherever you are! Wake up, everyone in Ibuza! . . . Girls, go and get the gong!'

The gong was large, shaped like a bell. When anyone hit it with a stick, it made a great deal of noise. As the first wife of the family, it was Ngbeke's duty to bang the gong. She had to tell the terrible news to the whole village.

Now everyone was screaming and crying. 'They shall die for this!' shouted Ngbeke's son Iloba. The noise was terrible.

Ma Blackie cried and cried. 'They have kidnapped my daughter,' she thought. 'Was it for this that I sent her to school? Kidnapped!'

The big boys went out to search for the kidnappers, Nna-nndo stopped crying and followed them. Ngbeke with her gong led the women around the village.

'Who has stolen our daughter?' (Gong). 'Come out and tell us!' (Gong). But they knew it was useless. Aku-nna had gone. The kidnapper had only to cut a piece of her hair, then the kidnapped girl belonged to him for ever. He could force her to sleep with him, and if she was unwilling, his friends could hold her down. Perhaps that had already happened to Aku-nna . . .

Ngbeke shouted until her throat was sore. Okonkwo shouted until he felt thirsty. Then he sat down with a bottle of native whisky for company. It was much later, in the middle of the night, when three men from the Obidi family came to him.

'Your daughter Aku-nna is sleeping peacefully,' they said, 'on the bed that we made specially for her and her husband Okoboshi.'

There was nothing Okonkwo could do. The whisky had made him sleepy and confused. Together he and the Obidi men agreed on a small bride price for Aku-nna.

'After all,' the Obidis said, 'there's nothing special about her except her education, and all this modern education doesn't do women any good . . . it makes them too proud.'

More whisky flowed. At last the three men prepared to leave. 'By morning,' they said, 'we shall know if she is a virgin or not.'

'She is a virgin,' said Okonkwo. 'Nobody has touched her. You must bring me a big pot full of wine.'

That was the tradition. If a bride was a virgin, her new family had to bring her father wine. If she was not a virgin, they brought an empty pot.

Meanwhile Nna-nndo had found out where his sister was. He went to his only friend, the only person who would never harm his sister. Then he went home and told Ma Blackie.

'Chike will save her,' he told her. But they both wondered how Chike could do that.

10

The Escape

Aku-nna was carried into her new home, and the women laid her on a bed. 'How smooth her body is!' they cried. 'How soft her hands are!'

When she became conscious again, Okoboshi's mother greeted her warmly. 'Don't worry. We'll send a message to your mother. You're in good hands. My husband decided to kidnap you for our boy because of that slave, Chike. No girl from a good family like yours could possibly marry a slave.'

'Oh no,' repeated the other women. 'Never!'

They showed Aku-nna a pile of new clothes. 'Look,' they

said. 'All these are for you.' They took off her short dancing skirt and tied a new skirt round her waist.

Then they took her into a room with a new, colourfully painted bed. 'For you and Okoboshi,' they explained.

They saw the fear and dislike on her face, and laughed. 'Don't worry,' said Okoboshi's mother. 'He'll be gentle with you. You may even like it – lots of girls do!'

The others laughed. They were very pleased with their new bride. But the bride herself was silent and trembling with fear.

'What's the matter?' demanded Okoboshi's eldest sister. 'Doesn't she like us?'

'Be quiet!' said her mother. 'No girl likes to be kidnapped. Go and join in the celebrations.'

Soon most of them left. But many visitors came to see the new bride. The men outside went on drinking whisky and firing guns for a long time. Aku-nna was stiff and tired, but she would not lie down.

'I'll die before I lie on that bed,' she thought.

Okoboshi's sister brought her some water. 'Would you like to wash?' she asked her.

'No, thank you,' said Aku-nna, 'but I need the toilet.'

'I will show you. Now remember, don't make it hard for Okoboshi. If you do, he'll call for help, then the men will come in and hold you down. That's the custom.'

'If that happens to me,' thought Aku-nna, 'I'll kill myself.'

Then, on the way to the toilet, she heard a whistle. It was Chike's special song. So he knew, and was near! But she could not get away, because Okoboshi's sister was watching her.

She was led back to the hut like a prisoner. She lay down on the bed with her face to the wall, and shut her eyes.

After a troubled sleep she woke with the feeling that someone was watching her. As she opened her eyes, she saw Okoboshi. He was smiling a cruel, unfriendly smile and he smelt of whisky. Suddenly Aku-nna realized how much he hated her.

He tried to touch her, but she fought like a wild animal. 'I'm on my own,' she thought. 'No one can help me. I must look after myself.'

Okoboshi laughed and hit her in the mouth. Then he was on top of her. She kicked and scratched, but he was too strong for her. Then suddenly an idea came to her. She laughed like a mad woman, and shouted at him:

'Look at you, Okoboshi! Am I the only bride you can get – the girlfriend of a slave?'

Okoboshi let her go. Aku-nna continued: 'You think I am a virgin? I tell you, a better man has been here before you! I have slept with him many, many times. That afternoon in school, when you and your friends made me cry – that was our first time. But it didn't do my schoolwork any harm, did it? You failed your examination, but I passed!'

Okoboshi stood up. His mouth hung open. He looked at her as a man looks at a poisonous insect.

She went on and on. 'Even if you do sleep with me tonight, what then? If I have a child, how can you be sure that the child is yours? And believe me, I shall tell everyone in the village!'

'But you were unclean until two days ago. Your mother said so.'

63

'Oh yes, that's true. But today I heard my examination results. We celebrated my success together!'

She said to herself, 'Have I gone too far? What if his people have been watching me all day? Then they'll know that I'm lying.'

Okoboshi hit her across the face with all his strength. 'You dirty animal!' he shouted. 'Do you think I want to touch you now? Slave-girl!' He hit her again. 'I never really wanted you anyway! My father helped me to kidnap you because he hated Ofulue, your slave lover's father. But just wait! Soon I shall marry the girl of my choice, and you will fetch and carry for her! Now get out of my bed!'

He hit her once more. She fell onto the floor and lost consciousness.

When she woke, it was almost morning. Okoboshi was asleep in the bridal bed. She ached all over. Just then Okoboshi woke and gave a cruel laugh.

'You'll have a busy day today, my educated bride. Go and find a gourd to take to the stream. The older women will ask you what happened. You'll have to tell them your story yourself. My father and I will go to your parents with an empty wine pot. Then the whole village will know about you and your slave lover!'

Aku-nna ran out of the hut, almost into the arms of Okoboshi's mother and sister. Okoboshi then came out and, with hate in his voice, he told them what Aku-nna had said the night before.

'So now **you** are a slave too! Well, the water gourds are there!' Okoboshi's mother said coldly.

As Aku-nna bent to pick up a gourd, Okoboshi's sister

'You can fetch and carry water for us – slave-girl!'

spoke: 'Mother, have you got an old skirt for this slave-girl? I need this one!' She tore the new skirt off Aku-nna's body. Her mother produced a dirty, torn skirt and stood there while Aku-nna tied it around her waist.

Then Aku-nna went to fetch the water, while everyone laughed and pointed. Her whole face was stiff and sore and she moved like an old woman. 'This is the end,' she thought. 'Now Chike will turn me away too. Okoboshi did not cut a piece of my hair last night. Why should he? I am worthless. I can run away if I want to, but where can I go? My uncle will kill me if I go home. But I'll die if I stay here. And when I die, they will say, "There, I told you so. She broke our laws. And now she is dead."'

All that morning Aku-nna was a prisoner in the hut of Okoboshi's mother. They gave her some cooked yam, but she could not eat it because her mouth was too sore and swollen.

At noon she heard a voice outside the hut. It was Nna-nndo. Okoboshi's mother let him see his sister alone. He brought her words of comfort – and a letter from Chike, which she read eagerly.

'Dearest,' it said, 'I will whistle after dark, when you go to the toilet. I love you. Chike.'

She gave the letter back to Nna-nndo, who hid it inside his shirt – just before Okoboshi marched into the room.

'So you have come to visit this slave-girl,' he said. He raised his hand and moved towards Aku-nna.

'If you touch my sister I'll kill you!' shouted Nna-nndo. He picked up a heavy pot. When Okoboshi's mother heard the shouting, she rushed in, took the pot from Nna-nndo and ordered him and her son to leave. Tears of anger poured down Nna-nndo's face as he left the hut.

Okoboshi's mother turned to Aku-nna. 'Go to Okoboshi tonight,' she said. 'Soon, perhaps, he will forgive you and take you into his bed. Many good marriages start unhappily.'

She was unexpectedly kind, and for a moment Aku-nna wanted to tell her the truth. But she remembered Chike's letter.

'I will go to him,' she said. 'Let me wash and go to the toilet first.'

As Aku-nna walked to the toilet, she suddenly heard Chike's whistle. There was a movement in the long grass, and before she knew what was happening, she was in Chike's arms. Then she heard his voice, low and urgent. 'Come on, my love – run!'

His warm body seemed to breathe new life into her. She ran. When she could no longer run, she walked. It was only seven miles from Ibuza to Asaba, but it took them nearly four hours. At last they reached a house.

'Our driver lives here,' said Chike. 'He'll take us to Ughelli in the morning.'

But Aku-nna was already asleep in Chike's arms.

11

Too Good to be True?

Ben Adegor was an old school friend of Chike's. They had written to each other regularly and Ben knew about Chike's feelings for Aku-nna. It was Ben who had suggested a job for Chike with the oil company at Ughelli, where Ben was the head teacher at the local school. Ben knew that the oil company needed bright young men, and he also promised to get Aku-nna a teaching job in his school.

'You and your bride can have my old hut until you find somewhere better,' he had written to Chike. 'I've bought a new house with a tin roof.'

Ben Adegor was a small, strong, dark man who loved to talk and argue. His wife Rose, who was small and dark too, was a teacher at the same school, and she was expecting their first child.

They welcomed Chike and Aku-nna kindly and showed them the hut with its three large rooms and its wide, airy veranda. They lent them some furniture, then left the young couple alone. Chike and Aku-nna stood and looked at each other.

'Will you marry me?' Chike whispered.

'Where you go, I go,' said Aku-nna.

Like small, excited children, they began to count their money. Chike's father had encouraged him to run away with Aku-nna and had given them a wedding present of a hundred pounds.

'I've never seen so much money before,' whispered Aku-nna, staring at Chike's hundred pounds.

'He was going to use it to pay for me to go to university,' said Chike.

'And you changed your plans?'

'Universities don't run away. I'll go when I'm ready. Just now I'm too busy. Guess what Father said when he gave me this money?'

'Did he tell you to pay my bride price with it?' asked Aku-nna with trembling lips.

He took her in his arms. 'Don't worry. My father will pay the bride price in good time. He will give Okonkwo double whatever he asks. But that isn't all. Nna-nndo must come and live with us, and get a proper education. Also we must send a little money to your mother, so that she can be independent.'

'Oh – will you do all that for me? I'll serve you until I die. I'll be a good wife to you. I'll always love you and love you, in this world and the next world, until the end of time.'

He kissed her hair. 'People will say you're marrying me because of my money!'

'Oh no, not because of that. Because of so many, many things – how can I name them all? Because of the way you look at me, because of your kindness and understanding . . .' Chike held her tight.

They had had very little sleep after their night's adventures, but now they forgot their tiredness. Chike wanted to go to town to do some shopping, and Aku-nna wanted to go with him.

'My father gave me this money to buy something special.

I'll buy it today, and tonight we'll christen it,' he told her.

The 'something special' was a lovely new English bed with a wonderfully soft mattress. Aku-nna clapped her hands with excitement when she saw it.

But their shopping did not end with the bed. Chike bought sheets, curtains, cooking pots and plates and even a small oil stove. Aku-nna had never seen anything like them before. He also bought her two beautiful new skirts.

'Thank you, thank you,' she said again and again.

They loaded everything onto a lorry. On the way home, Chike asked the driver to stop at the offices of the oil company.

'I'll only be away ten minutes,' he said. 'I want to tell them that I'm in Ughelli and available for an interview.'

Chike was away half an hour and came back looking pleased and proud. 'Sorry to keep you waiting,' he said to the driver. To Aku-nna he said, 'I start work in five days' time.'

Aku-nna could not believe it. 'Everything has been too easy for us,' she thought. 'It's too good to be true. Dear God, don't let anything happen to destroy our joy.'

Chike gave the driver a bottle of whisky and the driver wished them a long and happy marriage. When they unloaded the new bed in front of their new home, the driver poured a little whisky over the mattress.

'There, I have christened your bed,' he said. 'But you'll do it properly tonight, when you're alone!'

Then Chike's friend, Ben Adegor, came along and joined in the fun. 'So you're christening the bed?' he said. 'What are you going to call it?'

Aku-nna burst out laughing. 'Whoever heard of christening a bed?' she said.

But Ben was suddenly serious. He asked God to look kindly on his friends' marriage. 'Give them a happy life together, with many children. Now, I christen this bed Joy!'

But to Chike's surprise love-making did not come easily to them. At first Aku-nna tried to avoid it. First she wanted a bath, then she wanted to listen to their new radio . . . always she found some excuse. As for Chike, he was worried. When he had rescued her from Okoboshi, everything had seemed so easy. 'No matter what they have done to her, I will still marry her,' he thought. 'Even if she is expecting Okoboshi's child.'

He had discussed it with his father and the old man had given him some good advice. 'Never blame a woman for something that happened in the past,' he had said. 'It's the future that matters.'

But now Chike was anxious. Aku-nna seemed so frightened and worried. He wondered what they had done to her that night, and if she was still a virgin, but he did not want to ask her.

At last, however, Aku-nna told him her story. She told him that she was still a virgin, and that she had told lies to Okoboshi to get away from him.

'I have been saving myself for you,' she said shyly. 'Please help me to give you joy.'

Chike was surprised and delighted. 'My darling,' he said, 'your people must know of this. They must be told that you are innocent. My father must be told too. How happy they will all be!'

'*I christen this bed Joy!*'

'Is that necessary?' said Aku-nna. 'You know the truth, and that's all that matters. Just give them their bride price in peace. You know what they say: if the bride price is not paid, the bride will die in childbirth . . .' Aku-nna stopped for a moment. 'I love you, Chike,' she said softly. 'Please teach me . . .'

And the beautiful new bed became a place of joy for them both.

12

The Unpaid Price

In Ibuza there was no joy for Aku-nna's family. As soon as Okoboshi realized that Aku-nna had escaped with his enemy, he lied to his parents.

'I slept with her,' he said, 'and she was no virgin. But I cut off a piece of her hair, so now she belongs to me!' He produced a piece of hair to prove his story.

His action caused some bitter arguments, and many people became really angry with Chike's family. 'Who are they,' people said, 'to destroy the life of an innocent young girl? She will never come home to Ibuza now.'

'But,' said an old man, 'as long as Okonkwo does not accept any bride price from Ofulue, the girl still belongs to Okoboshi. No one can possibly expect a slave to behave like a free man, and no one can blame the girl if a slave runs off with her.'

The argument went on and on. Everyone spoke against

Chike's family. Ofulue did not fear for his own life, but he sent all the girls of the family away for a while. However, the people took their revenge in another way.

Years before, when Ofulue left his job as a head teacher, he had bought some land in Ibuza. He had planted trees there and looked after them well. Now one morning he woke up and found that all his trees had been cut down. The shock hurt the old man badly, and he was sure that Okoboshi's family, the Obidis, were responsible. Ofulue's sons were very angry, so together they collected enough money to take the Obidi family to law.

Everyone in Ibuza spoke against the Ofulue family, but the white man's law did not understand about slaves and free men. So the Obidi family were found guilty and the free men had to plant new trees for the slaves, and pay a large sum of money too. The Obidi family hated the Ofulue family more than ever after that, and naturally they saw Okonkwo's family as the cause of their misfortune, since Aku-nna was Okonkwo's responsibility.

All this had a very bad effect on Okonkwo, who felt that Aku-nna had behaved very badly and brought shame on the whole village. He became very ill, but the medicine men were unsympathetic.

'What do you expect?' they demanded. 'All this is your own fault.'

Okonkwo forgot about becoming a chief. He was fighting for his life and the life of his family. He blamed Ma Blackie for his troubles, and he took his revenge by divorcing her. After that, of course, everyone blamed Aku-nna.

*

In Ibuza, if you wanted to destroy someone, you made a little doll exactly like that person. Then you pushed a sharp needle into the doll's heart. The magic usually worked; the enemy died slowly and painfully.

Ma Blackie was sad, but not surprised, when one day she saw a little doll in Okonkwo's hut. The doll had Aku-nna's face, and there was a needle through its heart. She cried quietly for her daughter.

Chike and Aku-nna had sent a secret message to Ma Blackie, asking her to send her son Nna-nndo to Ughelli to live with them. Soon, too, the Ofulue family started sending Ma Blackie two whole pounds every month, which made her completely independent. 'I will pay a medicine man to destroy Okonkwo's magic,' she thought. 'Then my daughter will be safe.'

In Ughelli Aku-nna and Chike were wonderfully happy. After their wedding in the white man's church they moved to a small house of their own, quite near Ben and Rose Adegor. Aku-nna was teaching in the local school and Nna-nndo was doing well and growing like a young tree. The lorry driver who had christened their bed was now a useful friend and helper. Chike was training to become a manager of the oil company, and they had plenty of money.

Aku-nna was not always happy, however. Sometimes there was a shadow of sadness on her face, and Chike knew she was thinking about her bride price.

Chike's family wanted to pay it, but Okonkwo refused to accept the money. 'No girl in my family shall be the bride of a slave,' he said angrily.

'Don't worry,' Ofulue wrote to his son, 'I'll offer them more next time, and sooner or later they will accept.'

Chike told Aku-nna this sad news as gently as he could. She cried a little, because she knew that until the bride price was paid, her family would not recognize the marriage, and she was worried.

Ofulue soon learned about Okonkwo's little doll. He wrote and told Chike, but told him not to mention it to Aku-nna. 'It's only an old native tradition. If Aku-nna knows nothing about the doll, it cannot harm her.'

One day Chike came home from work and found Nna-nndo waiting for him. 'Where is Aku-nna?' demanded Chike. Usually she came running to greet him.

'She came back early from school with a headache,' said Nna-nndo. 'She's asleep now.'

Aku-nna looked very small and childlike on the big bed. Nna-nndo was growing every day, but his sister looked smaller and thinner than ever. She got tired very easily too. Chike went and sat down on the bed beside her. He touched her burning hot forehead. She opened her eyes and said, 'I'm sorry I wasn't there to welcome you home. I don't feel very well.'

'Is it that other pain?' he asked gently.

'No – I haven't had that since Christmas . . .'

'But that was three months ago, my love . . . Are you going to have a baby?'

'Perhaps!' she laughed. 'Mrs Adegor said the same thing this afternoon when she brought me home from school. I hope she's right, because I want to have your baby . . . Would you like that too?'

'Of course.' With her feverish head on his shoulder he talked to her about the baby. 'What shall we call our son?' he asked her.

'Will you be very disappointed if it's a girl?' asked Aku-nna.

'Not at all. But then people will talk. You know what people say about girl babies. They say girls are love babies. Their parents make love day and night. I want our love to be private!'

Aku-nna laughed. 'I'll ask God for a girl, then, and another one, and another one after that. Then everybody will know just how much we love each other . . . I'll have a son when you're forty.'

'You are a bad girl!' He kissed her.

Then he questioned her. Her tiredness worried him. Was it because of the baby, or because of her busy life? He decided that she ought to see a doctor.

The doctor at the oil company examined Aku-nna. 'Yes, she's going to have a baby,' he said. 'She must stop work and eat plenty of good food. Mr Ofulue, your wife is very young and small. Is she sixteen yet?'

'Yes,' said Chike. He felt suddenly very guilty. 'Will she be all right?'

'Oh, yes, but you must both be very careful. She isn't strong.'

Chike drove his wife home from the doctor's office in his new car. He drove badly and seemed annoyed with everything and everybody. Aku-nna wondered what was the matter, but she was too tired to talk. She fell asleep in the back of the car.

Aku-nna's wish to continue working was the cause of their first argument. 'I want to work, because you are sending money to my family,' she said.

Chike pushed her away. 'You mean you want to continue work until your bride price is paid,' he said unkindly. 'Why don't you say that? How many hours a day do you spend thinking about your family? You think about them so much, you forget about me. Don't you care about me? What if you become ill, too ill to look after our child? Listen, I'll make sure that your bride price is paid. And you're not going to die and leave me – do you understand?'

At the mention of dying Aku-nna was afraid. 'Am I going to die?' she thought. 'Did the doctor say that?' Aloud she said, 'Please tell me the truth. Did the doctor say I was going to die? Is that why you were so unhappy on the way home?'

He took her in his arms. 'No, no, he didn't say anything like that. I was just expressing my own fears. But he did say we had to be careful. You must rest. Dearest, I don't want anything to happen to you. You mean so much to me.'

13

Joy

Soon Aku-nna was glad to stay at home. The baby was giving her a very bad time. In the early months she was sick every morning and unable to eat. Even in the sixth month, she still could not enjoy her food. She hated to cause her young husband so much worry. Chike remained gentle and loving with her, but his eyes were large and anxious. He paid a local girl to clean the house and do the cooking. 'Take it easy,' he said to Aku-nna. 'Read as much as you like, and eat plenty of good food.'

Chike's eldest brother, who was a doctor, visited them and examined Aku-nna. 'She's not strong,' he told Chike.

'What's the matter with her?' demanded Chike. 'Most girls in Ibuza have babies very easily. Why is it so hard for my wife? She's getting weaker every day.'

'Don't worry. We can always take her into the hospital for an operation, and save both her and the child. And do remember that many native girls die in childbirth too. Your wife didn't get enough of the right food when she was young. She's sixteen, but she looks like a fourteen-year-old. You were wrong to give her a child so early, brother.'

Chike gave a short, bitter laugh. 'We didn't plan this baby – it just happened.'

'Don't worry, everything will be all right. You're a lucky man. She's a sweet, lovely girl. Take good care of her now.'

At home in Ibuza, Ofulue again asked Okonkwo to accept the bride price, and again Okonkwo refused to give his daughter to a slave. Then one day somebody – nobody knew who – took away the little doll from Okonkwo's hut. Okonkwo was terribly angry. He paid a medicine man a lot of money to make a new doll. 'This will bring Aku-nna home,' he said. 'It will call her back in the wind.'

Chike's father came to Ughelli to visit them, and was very glad to see them so happy. When Chike was at work, Ofulue

79

and Aku-nna talked and laughed together like old friends. But he always reminded her to rest, so that she was fresh and happy when she welcomed Chike home from the office.

When it was time for Ofulue to leave, Aku-nna cried on his shoulder. 'I hope I shall see you again, Father. I know that my uncle Okonkwo does not want to accept my bride price. He hates me. He's calling me back. I hear his voice in the wind when I'm alone – but I'll never answer him . . . Oh, Father, I don't want to die!'

Chike did not hear Aku-nna's words, but he knew she was crying. He came over and took her gently away from his father. 'After our baby is born,' he told her, 'we shall all go home together and visit Father. We'll all look forward to that.'

Aku-nna tried to smile as she waved goodbye to her father-in-law. But now she was frightened to be alone. Again and again she heard her uncle's voice calling her, telling her to return to her family. She could no longer sleep. The doctor gave her sleeping tablets, but they did not help.

Every night she and Chike knelt down together and asked God to help them through this difficult time, but still Aku-nna could not rest. Sometimes she woke in the night, crying. 'Hold me tight!' she begged Chike. 'Hold me! My uncle is trying to take me away. Please don't let him get me.'

'Don't be silly,' said Chike gently. 'You don't really believe all that nonsense, do you? You're anxious and excited, that's all. Cheer up; soon the baby will be here.' Gently he rubbed her tight, swollen stomach, which looked so huge beside her thin little arms and legs.

'*My uncle Okonkwo won't accept my bride price. He hates me. He's calling me back. I hear his voice in the wind . . .*'

They spent many nights like this. Then one night Aku-nna suddenly screamed and lost consciousness. Chike examined her; the baby was coming. At once he telephoned the doctor, who sent an ambulance at once.

Chike watched anxiously while the ambulance men covered his wife with their horrible red blankets and lifted her into the ambulance. Then he sat beside her and held her hand. When the pains stabbed through her body, he felt them too.

When they reached the hospital, the doctor told him the truth. 'She must have an operation,' he said. 'The baby is small, but it will be all right.'

As Chike sat on the hard chair in the hospital waiting-room, he remembered the shy little girl from Lagos. He remembered all their happy times . . . the day they bought their new bed, the day he received his first cheque from the oil company. He remembered their escape together and tears poured down his face.

Someone touched his shoulder. It was Nna-nndo, who had ridden the seven miles to the hospital on his bicycle, to sit beside his brother-in-law. To Nna-nndo, Chike was perfect. He loved him and was grateful to him for his happy life in Ughelli. He wanted to help Chike, but did not know how. He held Chike's hand and cried.

A doctor came in. 'Mr Ofulue?' he said. 'Please come with me.'

Chike followed like a sleepwalker. The doctor said, 'She has had the operation. She isn't conscious yet, and I'm afraid that she may never wake up at all. I'm sorry – we did everything we could, but she was very small and weak. I don't know how she stayed alive so long . . . I expect you want to sit with her. She's in here.' He pointed to a door. 'By the way,' he whispered, 'you have a baby girl. She's small, but she's doing fine.'

Chike stared wordlessly at the doctor, then he went into the unnaturally clean white room. He was alone with Aku-nna.

She was so beautiful and peaceful lying there. He took her small, dry hand and held it. Aku-nna was dying. Chike called Nna-nndo, and the two of them sat there together.

It was almost morning when Aku-nna's hand moved a little. There was a smile on her lips, and she spoke softly but clearly.

'I know you are here, my husband.' Slowly she opened her eyes. They were very bright, too bright for this world. Nna-nndo heard her voice and came nearer.

'Don't worry, brother,' she said. 'This isn't the end of the road for you, it's the beginning. My husband will look after you. He's a good man, and I thank God for him.'

Nna-nndo began to cry. Then Aku-nna spoke to Chike. 'Dear husband, be strong. Be happy for me.' Her voice was very weak now. 'Did we have a boy or a girl?'

'A little girl,' he whispered in her ear.

Aku-nna's whole face shone with joy. 'I told you so,' she whispered. 'I told you I wouldn't keep our love a secret. Now everybody will see our little girl, and they will know that our love will never die . . . Let's call her "Joy" too, the same name that we gave our marriage bed. Please. Promise me you'll call her Joy . . . Then promise me that you'll be happy, because you have made me so happy, so . . .

'*Promise me that you'll be happy, Chike, because you have made me so happy . . .*'

Her eyes closed. Chike took her whole body in his arms and kissed her gently. 'Good night, my love. Our child's name shall be Joy.'

She smiled again, a smile of unbelievable sweetness and beauty. Very softly and peacefully, she died. But he still held her gently, lovingly against his heart.

The morning light grew stronger. The doctor came in. 'It is time to go now,' he said. 'Your wife is at peace.'

'Our child shall be called Joy,' repeated Chike.

Afterwards every girl in Ibuza was told the sad story of Aku-nna and Chike. 'If you want to live a long time,' they were told, 'you must accept the husband that your people choose for you, and your bride price must be paid. If it is not paid, you will never survive the birth of your first child.'

Of course, that is all nonsense. Of course a safe birth does not depend on a bride price. But even today, no girl wants to risk it.

GLOSSARY

aja   A Nigerian word for a special kind of dance
birth   the act or time of being born
cassava   an African vegetable from which bread can be made
childbirth   the act of giving birth to a child
christen   to give a name to someone or something
Christian   someone who believes in Jesus Christ
come to no good   to get into trouble or have a bad life
comfort *(v)*   to give help, kindness, etc. to someone who is unhappy
degree   a certificate given by a university
doll   a toy in the shape of a person
funeral   the ceremony when a dead person is buried
gong   a round piece of metal which makes a loud ringing noise
   when it is beaten
gourd   a large, hollow fruit with a hard skin, sometimes used for
   carrying liquids
gradually   happening slowly and evenly (not suddenly)
graveyard   a place where dead people are buried
houseboy   a boy or young man in Nigeria who works as a servant
   for his relations
hut   a house made of wood and grass or leaves
inherit   to receive money or other things which belonged to
   someone who has died
ink   a black or coloured liquid used for writing
join in   to take part in something as a member of a group
joy   great happiness
kidnap *(v)*   to take someone away and keep them prisoner
longingly   showing a very strong wish
Ma   mother (a name usually used by children)

marry somebody off to arrange a marriage for somebody (usually a daughter)

mattress a large, flat bag filled with something soft, used on a bed for sleeping on

medicine man an African doctor who uses magic to harm people or to make them well

mourn to cry and be sad for someone who has died

native belonging to the place or country where a person was born (in this story African, not European)

nut a fruit with a very hard skin

Obi a Nigerian word for a chief (a head man)

ogbanje a Nigerian word meaning 'living dead' (a person who is alive but not very healthy)

operation the cutting of the body by a doctor in order to remove or mend something in a sick person

powerful very strong or important

respect *(n)* behaving politely towards someone older or more important

respect *(v)* to show respect for somebody

scholarship money given to a clever person to pay for his or her education

shame *(n)* blame and bad opinions caused by somebody's bad behaviour

shilling a silver coin in Nigerian money

shot *(n)* the firing of a gun

slave a servant who is owned by another person and who can be bought and sold

sociology the study of societies and human behaviour

spirit the part of a person that is not the body; some people believe the spirit lives after the body dies

stove   something which produces heat for cooking on (in this story a wood fire in a fireplace)

strength   being strong

suspicious   having a feeling that something is wrong

swell (past participle **swollen**)   to become filled with liquid and/or air and become larger

tablet   a solid medicine, usually in small round pieces

tradition   a custom or habit which has been followed for many years

veranda   a long, open platform with a roof along the outside of a house

virgin   a girl who has not yet been to bed with (made love with) a man

waste *(v)*   to spend or use something (e.g. money or time) in a useless way

yam   a vegetable, a little like a potato

The Bride Price

ACTIVITIES

Before Reading

1 Read the story introduction on the first page of the book, and the back cover. What do you know now about Aku-nna? Circle the correct words in this passage.

When Aku-nna's *mother / father* dies, she has to leave *Lagos / Ibuza* and goes to live in *the capital / her hometown*. She is an *innocent / experienced* girl, who finds her new life *easy / difficult*, especially as her *sister / brother* is too *young / busy* to give her any *money / advice*. At first she has *several / no* friends, and so she feels very *lonely / lucky*, but soon she meets a *distant relation / young man*, who is *kind / unpleasant* to her.

2 Read the story introduction and back cover again. Can you guess what might happen to Aku-nna in this story? Cross out the suggestions that you think are unlikely.

Aku-nna will . . .

1 continue her studies / have to leave school and do farm work / become a teacher.
2 marry the man she loves / marry a man she dislikes / never marry.
3 have many children / have only one child / not have any children.
4 be unhappy all her life / be happy all her life / be happy for a short time.
5 live a long time / die young / kill herself.

While Reading

Read Chapters 1 to 3. Are these sentences true (T) or false (F)? Rewrite the false sentences with the correct information.

1 Ma Blackie and Ezekiel did not mind that they only had two children.
2 Aku-nna's parents were proud of their strong, healthy daughter.
3 When Ezekiel went to the hospital for a check-up, he knew he might not see his children again.
4 Ma Blackie stayed in Ibuza during her husband's illness because she did not care about him.
5 Aku-nna shared the kitchen with fifteen other families.
6 Aku-nna guessed that her father had died before she was told.
7 Ezekiel's funeral combined native and Christian ceremonies.
8 The mourning for Ezekiel lasted for several days.
9 Aku-nna's aunts did not expect her to get a good bride price because she was a noisy, stupid girl.

Before you read Chapter 4 (*The Journey to Ibuza*), can you guess the answers to these questions?

1 Where will Aku-nna and her brother live now?
2 What will happen to Aku-nna and Nna-nndo if their mother remarries?
3 Will Aku-nna be married off, so that her bride price can pay for Nna-nndo's education?
4 Who will be the head of the family now – Ma Blackie, Nna-nndo, or somebody else?

Read Chapters 4 to 7. Who said this and to whom? What or who were they talking about?

1 'I don't want them to see you both looking dirty.'
2 'No nice girl from a good family is allowed to talk to him.'
3 'School is no use to a free man. School is a place to send your slaves.'
4 'Their bride prices will come to me, and these days, people pay more for educated girls.'
5 'They all die young, usually at the birth of their first child.'
6 'If she is, I will kill her.'
7 'I would not like a son of mine to bring shame on his daughter.'
8 'Surely she must be married one day?'
9 'You will always be mine.'
10 'There will be trouble.'

Before you read Chapter 8 (*Kidnapped!*), what do you think will happen next? Circle Y (Yes) or N (No) for each of these possibilities.

1 Ogugua will be kidnapped by Chike, to make her father agree to Chike's marrying Aku-nna. Y/N
2 Aku-nna will be kidnapped by the Obidi family, as a wife for Okoboshi. Y/N
3 Chike will kidnap Aku-nna, and they will run away together to get married. Y/N
4 Whoever is kidnapped will manage to escape and return home safely. Y/N
5 The people of Ibuza will force the kidnappers to let their prisoner go, and will punish the kidnappers. Y/N

Read Chapters 8 to 10. Choose the best question-word for these questions, and then answer them.

What / Who / Why

1 . . . did Okonkwo forbid Aku-nna to see Chike?
2 . . . knocked Okoboshi down in Ma Blackie's hut?
3 . . . was the *aja* dance so important to the girls of Ibuza?
4 . . . failed the school examination?
5 . . . did Ngbeke and the others go to Ma Blackie's hut?
6 . . . kidnapped Aku-nna?
7 . . . preparations had the Obidi family made for their son's wedding?
8 . . . did Aku-nna tell Okoboshi in order to prevent him making love to her?
9 . . . rescued Aku-nna from the Obidi family?

Before you read to the end of the story, what do you think is going to happen? Circle Y (Yes) or N (No) for each of these possibilities.

1 Aku-nna marries Chike and they have a long and happy life together, surrounded by their children. Y/N
2 Aku-nna marries Chike, but dies young in childbirth. Y/N
3 Aku-nna is forced to return to Okoboshi, and lives unhappily with him for the rest of her life. Y/N
4 Chike still loves Aku-nna, but cannot marry her because she now belongs to Okoboshi. Y/N
5 Chike soon leaves Aku-nna for another girl, so Aku-nna decides to become a teacher and lead an independent life. Y/N

How would you *like* the story to end?

After Reading

1 **Perhaps this is what some of the characters in the story were thinking. Who are they, and what is happening in the story at this moment?**

1 'It's not the bride price I was hoping for. But what could I do? They've got the girl already, so I had to agree to what they offered. At least her husband won't be the son of a slave . . .'

2 'She's so quiet, so shy! And she doesn't know much about our customs. I suppose it's because she's lived in the city. Still, it's fun to have a new cousin. I think I'm going to like her . . .'

3 'He's certainly in love – buying good bananas and then just throwing them in the river! The things young lovers do! Well, he must marry her. I'll offer a good bride price, and I just hope there won't be too much trouble with her family . . .'

4 'I hate him! I'd like to kill him, I really would! How dare he hit my sister and call her names! But at least I showed her the letter and got it back inside my shirt before anyone came in.'

5 'What's this? Oh no! There's a needle through the heart. I was afraid he'd do something like this. How can I stop it? Yes – I've got the money now. I can pay someone to destroy it . . .'

6 'He'll be sorry for this! Who does he think he is? Knocking me down in front of everyone – *me*, a free man! I'm going to get my revenge on this slave somehow. I'll go home and talk to Father right now . . .'

2 When Ofulue first went to Okonkwo to ask for Aku-nna (see page 58), what did the two men say to each other? Complete Ofulue's side of the conversation.

OKONKWO: Well, Ofulue, what do you want with me?
OFULUE: _____
OKONKWO: My niece? What about her?
OFULUE: _____
OKONKWO: I don't care if he's in love or not. Marriage is a business matter, as you well know.
OFULUE: _____
OKONKWO: It will have to be a *very* good bride price. I'm hoping to become an *Obi* soon.
OFULUE: _____
OKONKWO: A hundred? Mmm . . .
OFULUE: _____
OKONKWO: I haven't agreed to anything yet. I'll think about it.

3 After his sister's kidnap, Nna-nndo went to see Chike (see page 61). Put their conversation in the right order, and write in the speakers' names. Begin with number 7.

1 _____ 'The Obidis won't stop me visiting my own sister!'
2 _____ 'Who cares about those old traditions? All I care about is Aku-nna. And I'm going to rescue her and take her away.'
3 _____ 'It was at the dancing hut. About twelve men broke in, put out all the oil lamps, and then carried my sister off.'
4 _____ 'I don't know yet. Listen, Nna-nndo, do you think you could get a message to Aku-nna?'
5 _____ 'But Chike – suppose Okoboshi's already cut off a piece of her hair? Then she'll belong to him for ever.'

6 _____ 'Good. I'll make a plan. Come back in the morning, and I'll give you a letter to take to Aku-nna.'

7 _____ 'Chike, Chike! Have you heard what's happened?'

8 _____ 'And now they'll try and force her to marry that horrible Okoboshi. But I won't let it happen!'

9 _____ 'Are you? Oh, Chike, that would be wonderful! But how will you do it?'

10 _____ 'Yes, the Obidis have kidnapped Aku-nna. I guessed when I heard the guns. How did it happen, Nna-nndo?'

4 **Imagine that Aku-nna wrote to Chike after the kidnap. Put her letter in the right order, and join the parts with the linking words, to make a paragraph of four sentences.**

and anyway / and then / because / but / in order to / that

Dear Chike,

1 There's no time to write any more,

2 _____ make me Okoboshi's bride.

3 _____ we must say goodbye,

4 Soon his father will pay Okonkwo a bride price for me,

5 _____ I cannot go against my people's traditions.

6 _____ I will have to stay here as Okoboshi's wife.

7 I expect you've heard by now

8 Chike, I shall always love you,

9 _____ the paper is too wet with my tears.

10 _____ the Obidis have kidnapped me,

Your loving Aku-nna

Aku-nna did not send a letter like this to Chike. Should she have done? What do *you* think?

5 **Ofulue wrote to Chike in Ughelli to tell him about the little doll in Okonkwo's hut (see page 76). Write his letter, by combining these sentences into longer sentences, using linking words and making any other necessary changes.**

Dear son,

I visited Okonkwo again recently.

I offered Okonkwo a much higher bride price for Aku-nna.

Okonkwo still refuses to accept the bride price.

Okonkwo talks wildly about Aku-nna.

Aku-nna, Okonkwo says, has brought shame on the whole village.

Okonkwo blames Aku-nna for all his troubles.

I also heard something from Ma Blackie.

You won't like this.

Okonkwo has a doll in his hut.

The doll has Aku-nna's face, and a needle through its heart.

Don't tell Aku-nna about the doll.

It's only the old women who believe in this kind of thing.

Aku-nna knows nothing about the doll.

The doll cannot possibly harm Aku-nna.

Take care of Aku-nna and yourself,

Your father

6 **Here are ten different titles for the story. Which do you like best? Put them in order of preference, 1 to 10 (number 1 for the best).**

Love and Tradition	Forbidden Love
Called Back in the Wind	A Slave's Bride
The Price of Love	Joy in the Morning
A Suitable Husband	Love Finds a Way
Parents Always Know Best	From City to Village

7 **Every girl in Ibuza was told the sad story of Aku-nna and Chike. Here is the story. Choose one suitable word to fill each gap.**

Listen carefully, because you must not _____ the same mistake Aku-nna made. Her _____, who as the head of the _____ was responsible for her, decided she _____ marry one of the Obidi family, _____ would pay a good bride price. _____ the girl grateful to her kind, _____ uncle for feeding and clothing her? _____! Did she politely agree to his _____? No! She thought she knew better _____ him, and so she wouldn't even _____ at the boy who wanted to _____ her. Instead, she spent all her _____ time with the son of a _____! You can imagine what her family _____ about that! One evening she was _____ by the Obidi family for their _____, and, foolish girl! she refused to _____ him as her husband. No, she _____ away with the slave's son, and _____ they did get married, no bride _____ was ever paid for her. And _____ of this, poor Aku-nna did not _____ the birth of her first child.

8 **How can Aku-nna's death be explained? Did it happen because of native tradition, or for medical reasons? Use these notes to write two different explanations.**

Native tradition
- unpaid bride price / doll with a needle in its heart / calling back in the wind / an *ogbanje* (living dead)

Medical reasons
- not eating properly in childhood / too small to have a baby naturally / not eating properly when pregnant / too weak to survive a serious operation

Which explanation do *you* think is the most likely? Why?

ABOUT THE AUTHOR

Florence Onye Buchi Emecheta was born to Igbo parents in a small village near Lagos, the capital of Nigeria, in 1944. She moved to Britain with her student husband in 1962, studied sociology at the University of London, and worked in a library and later as a community worker, while bringing up her five children. Her first novel was published in 1972, and since then she has written about twenty novels, as well as children's books and television plays. She has also been a teacher and visiting professor of English at several universities in the United States, Britain, and Nigeria. She lives in North London.

Emecheta is best known for her novels set in Nigeria both before and after independence, and her writing gives a powerful impression of what it means to be a woman and mother in Nigerian society. Her novels also reflect her own experience of life – *In the Ditch* (1972) and *Second-Class Citizen* (1974) describe the difficulties and hardships of her own early married life in Britain. *The Bride Price* (1976) and *The Joys of Motherhood* (1979) show how the traditions of African society affect the lives of women. But as Emecheta herself says, 'The main themes of my novels are African society and family; . . . I have not committed myself to the cause of African women only. I write about Africa as a whole.'

She sees herself as part of a long cultural line. 'Women are born storytellers. We keep the history . . . What I do is not clever or unusual. It is what my aunt and my grandmother did, and their mothers before them.'

OXFORD BOOKWORMS LIBRARY

Classics • Crime & Mystery • Factfiles • Fantasy & Horror
Human Interest • Playscripts • Thriller & Adventure
True Stories • World Stories

The OXFORD BOOKWORMS LIBRARY provides enjoyable reading in English, with a wide range of classic and modern fiction, non-fiction, and plays. It includes original and adapted texts in seven carefully graded language stages, which take learners from beginner to advanced level. An overview is given on the next pages.

All Stage 1 titles are available as audio recordings, as well as over eighty other titles from Starter to Stage 6. All Starters and many titles at Stages 1 to 4 are specially recommended for younger learners. Every Bookworm is illustrated, and Starters and Factfiles have full-colour illustrations.

The OXFORD BOOKWORMS LIBRARY also offers extensive support. Each book contains an introduction to the story, notes about the author, a glossary, and activities. Additional resources include tests and worksheets, and answers for these and for the activities in the books. There is advice on running a class library, using audio recordings, and the many ways of using Oxford Bookworms in reading programmes. Resource materials are available on the website <www.oup.com/bookworms>.

The *Oxford Bookworms Collection* is a series for advanced learners. It consists of volumes of short stories by well-known authors, both classic and modern. Texts are not abridged or adapted in any way, but carefully selected to be accessible to the advanced student.

You can find details and a full list of titles in the *Oxford Bookworms Library Catalogue* and *Oxford English Language Teaching Catalogues*, and on the website <www.oup.com/bookworms>.

THE OXFORD BOOKWORMS LIBRARY
GRADING AND SAMPLE EXTRACTS

STARTER • 250 HEADWORDS

present simple – present continuous – imperative –
can/cannot, must – *going to* (future) – simple gerunds ...

Her phone is ringing – but where is it?

Sally gets out of bed and looks in her bag. No phone. She looks under the bed. No phone. Then she looks behind the door. There is her phone. Sally picks up her phone and answers it. *Sally's Phone*

STAGE 1 • 400 HEADWORDS

... past simple – coordination with *and*, *but*, *or* –
subordination with *before*, *after*, *when*, *because*, *so* ...

I knew him in Persia. He was a famous builder and I worked with him there. For a time I was his friend, but not for long. When he came to Paris, I came after him – I wanted to watch him. He was a very clever, very dangerous man. *The Phantom of the Opera*

STAGE 2 • 700 HEADWORDS

... present perfect – *will* (future) – *(don't) have to, must not, could* –
comparison of adjectives – simple *if* clauses – past continuous –
tag questions – *ask/tell* + infinitive ...

While I was writing these words in my diary, I decided what to do. I must try to escape. I shall try to get down the wall outside. The window is high above the ground, but I have to try. I shall take some of the gold with me – if I escape, perhaps it will be helpful later. *Dracula*

STAGE 3 • 1000 HEADWORDS

... should, may – present perfect continuous – *used to* – past perfect –
causative – relative clauses – indirect statements ...

Of course, it was most important that no one should see
Colin, Mary, or Dickon entering the secret garden. So Colin
gave orders to the gardeners that they must all keep away
from that part of the garden in future. ***The Secret Garden***

STAGE 4 • 1400 HEADWORDS

... past perfect continuous – passive (simple forms) –
would conditional clauses – indirect questions –
relatives with *where/when* – gerunds after prepositions/phrases ...

I was glad. Now Hyde could not show his face to the world
again. If he did, every honest man in London would be proud
to report him to the police. ***Dr Jekyll and Mr Hyde***

STAGE 5 • 1800 HEADWORDS

... future continuous – future perfect –
passive (modals, continuous forms) –
would have conditional clauses – modals + perfect infinitive ...

If he had spoken Estella's name, I would have hit him. I was so
angry with him, and so depressed about my future, that I could
not eat the breakfast. Instead I went straight to the old house.
Great Expectations

STAGE 6 • 2500 HEADWORDS

... passive (infinitives, gerunds) – advanced modal meanings –
clauses of concession, condition

When I stepped up to the piano, I was confident. It was as if I
knew that the prodigy side of me really did exist. And when I
started to play, I was so caught up in how lovely I looked that
I didn't worry how I would sound. ***The Joy Luck Club***

Heat and Dust

RUTH PRAWER JHABVALA

Retold by Clare West

Heat and dust – these simple, terrible words describe the Indian summer. Year after year, endlessly, it is the same. And everyone who experiences this heat and dust is changed for ever.

We often say, in these modern times, that sexual relationships have changed, for better or for worse. But in this book we see that things have not changed. Whether we look back sixty years, or a hundred and sixty, we see that it is not things that change, but people. And, in the heat and dust of an Indian summer, even people are not very different after all.

The Age of Innocence

EDITH WHARTON

Retold by Clare West

Into the narrow social world of New York in the 1870s comes Countess Ellen Olenska, surrounded by shocked whispers about her failed marriage to a rich Polish Count. A woman who leaves her husband can never be accepted in polite society.

Newland Archer is engaged to young May Welland, but the beautiful and mysterious Countess needs his help. He becomes her friend and defender, but friendship with an unhappy, lonely woman is a dangerous path for a young man to follow – especially a young man who is soon to be married.